ANIMAL

Zentangles

AN ADULT COLORING BOOK

Vol. 1

Zhena Khasha

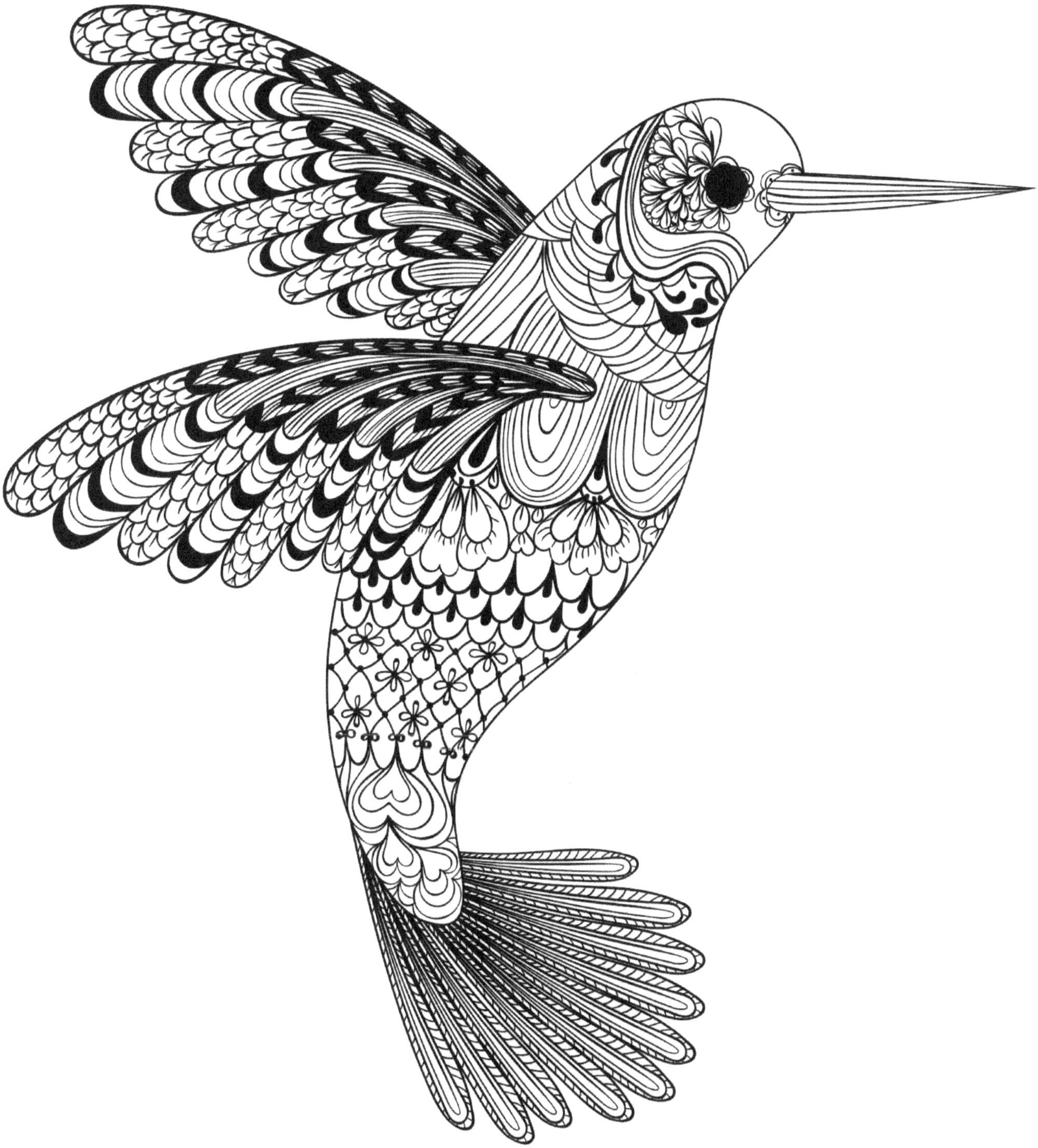

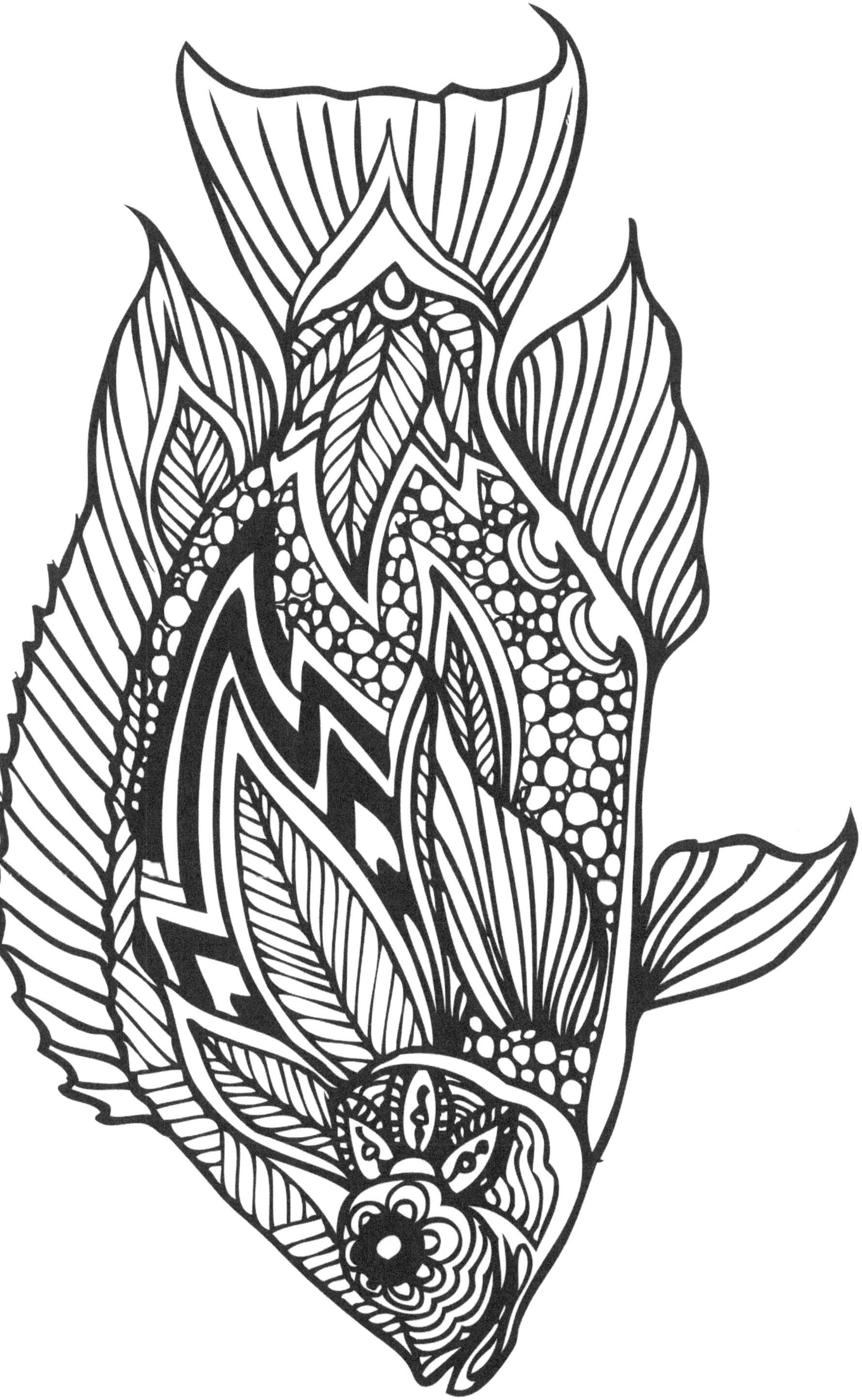

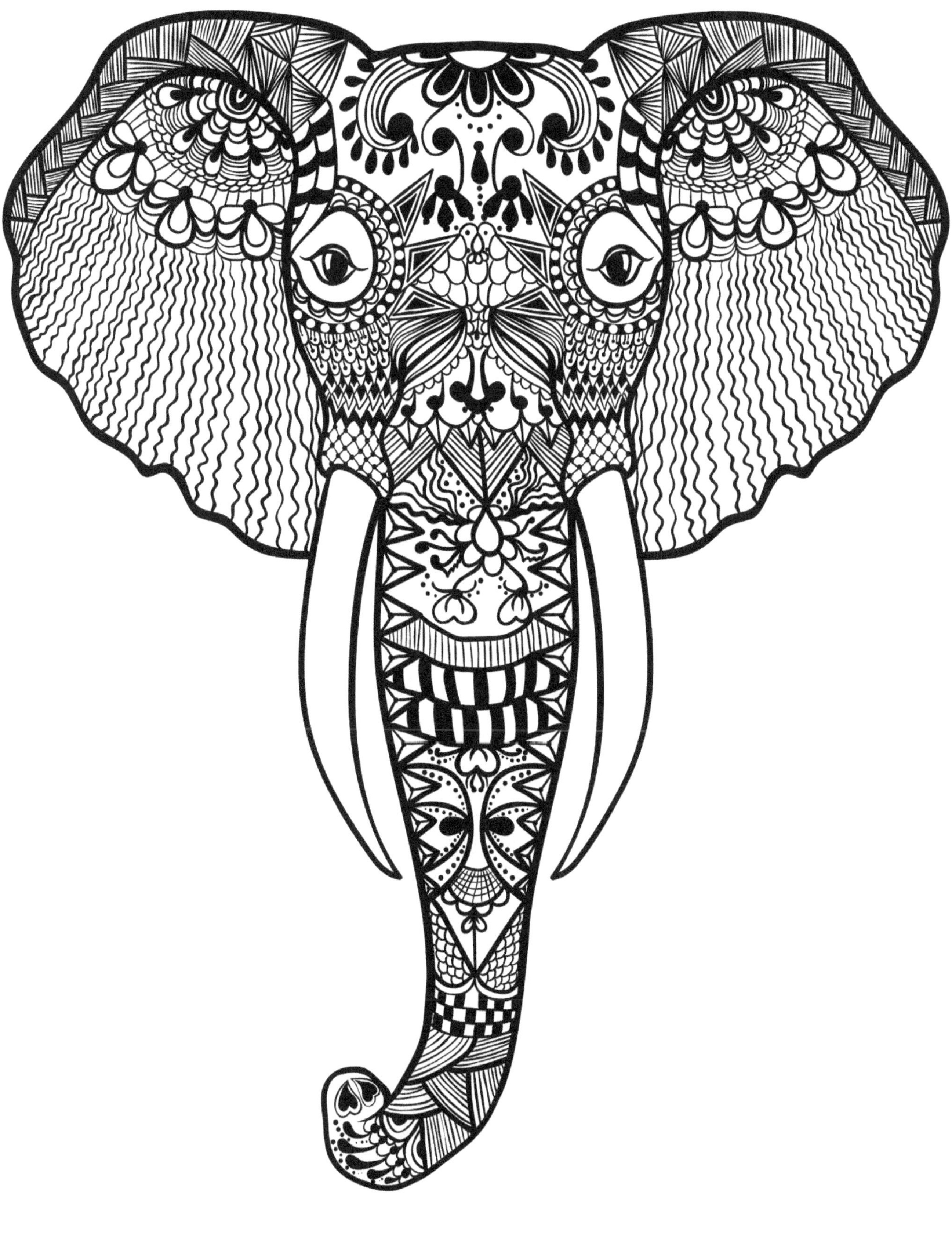

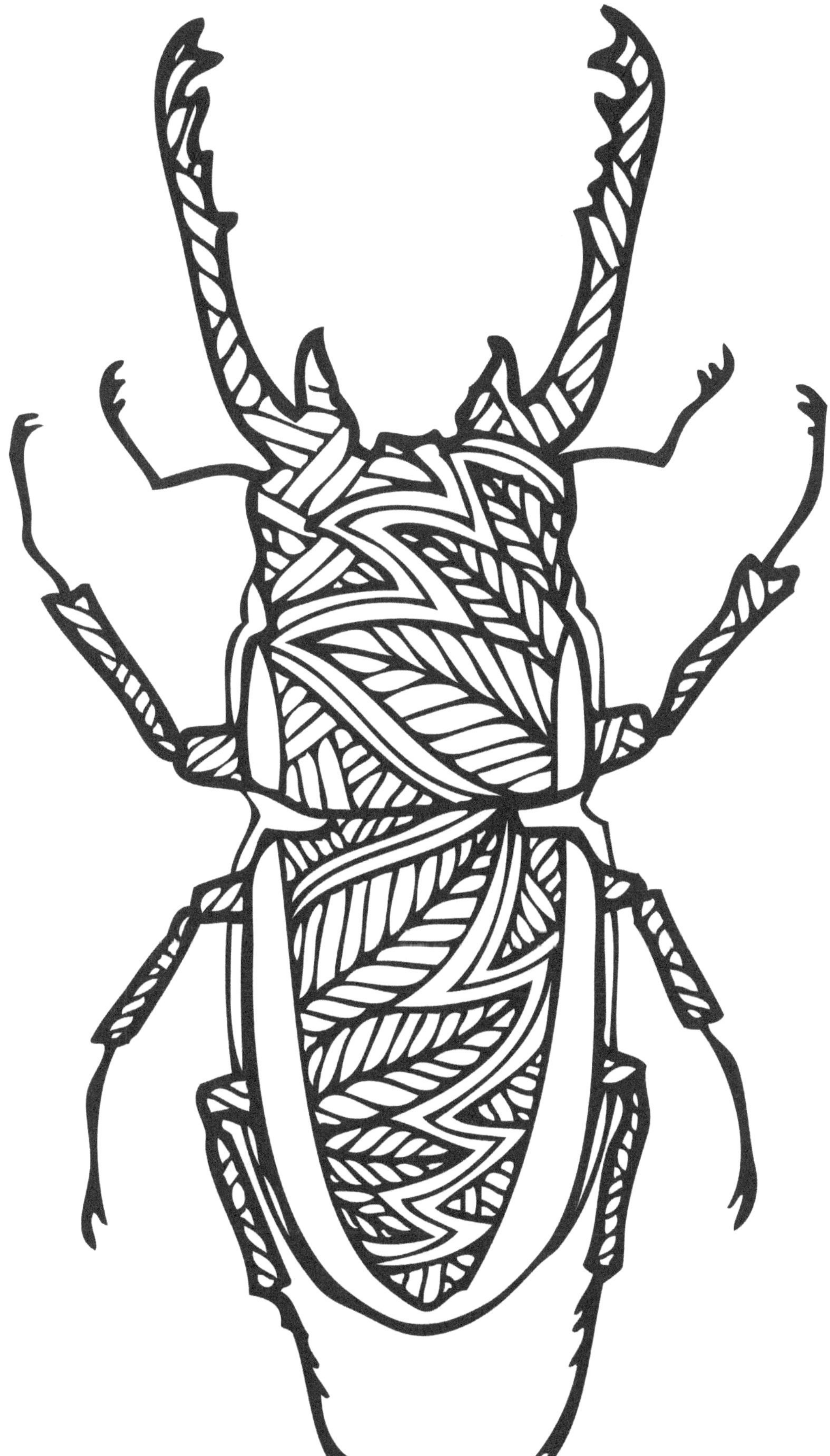

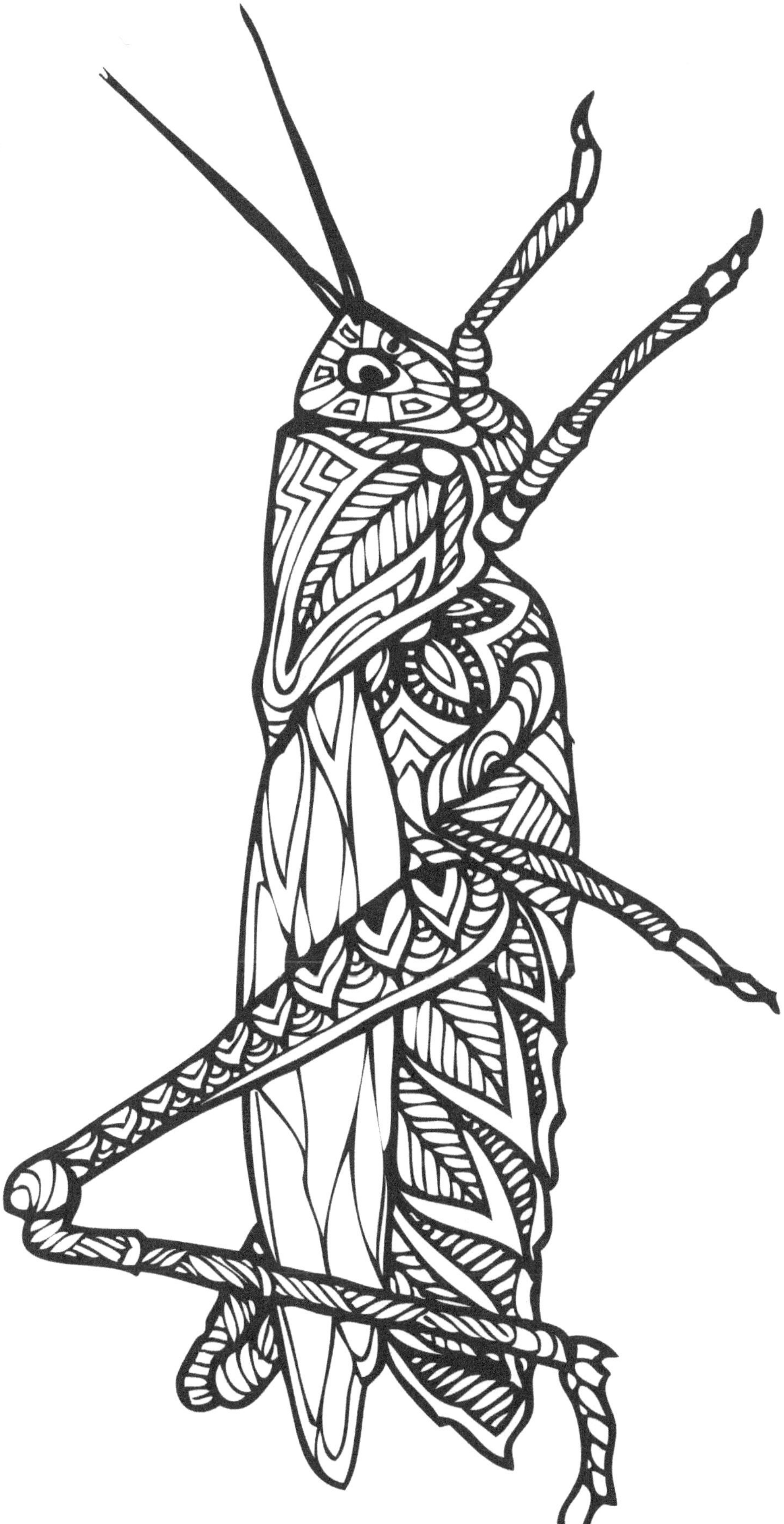

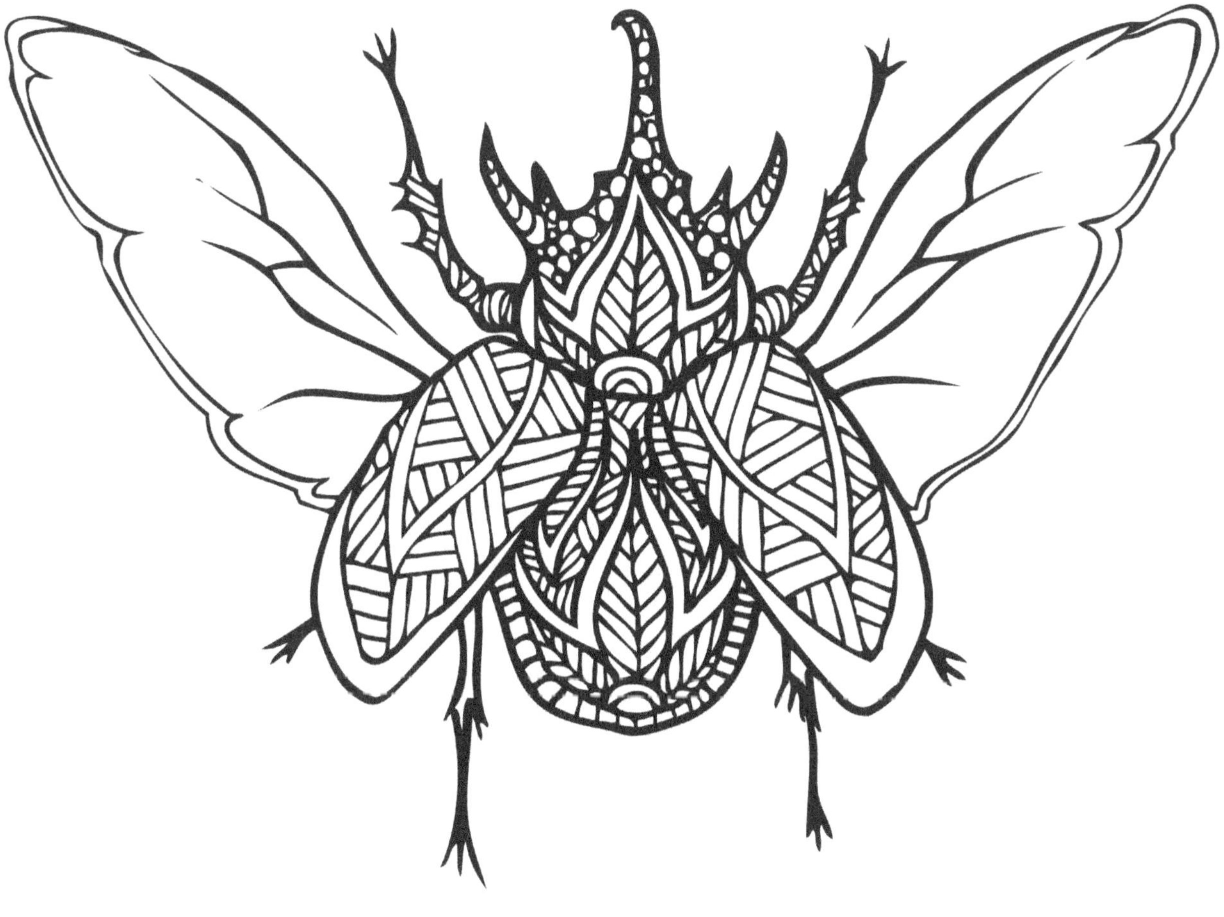

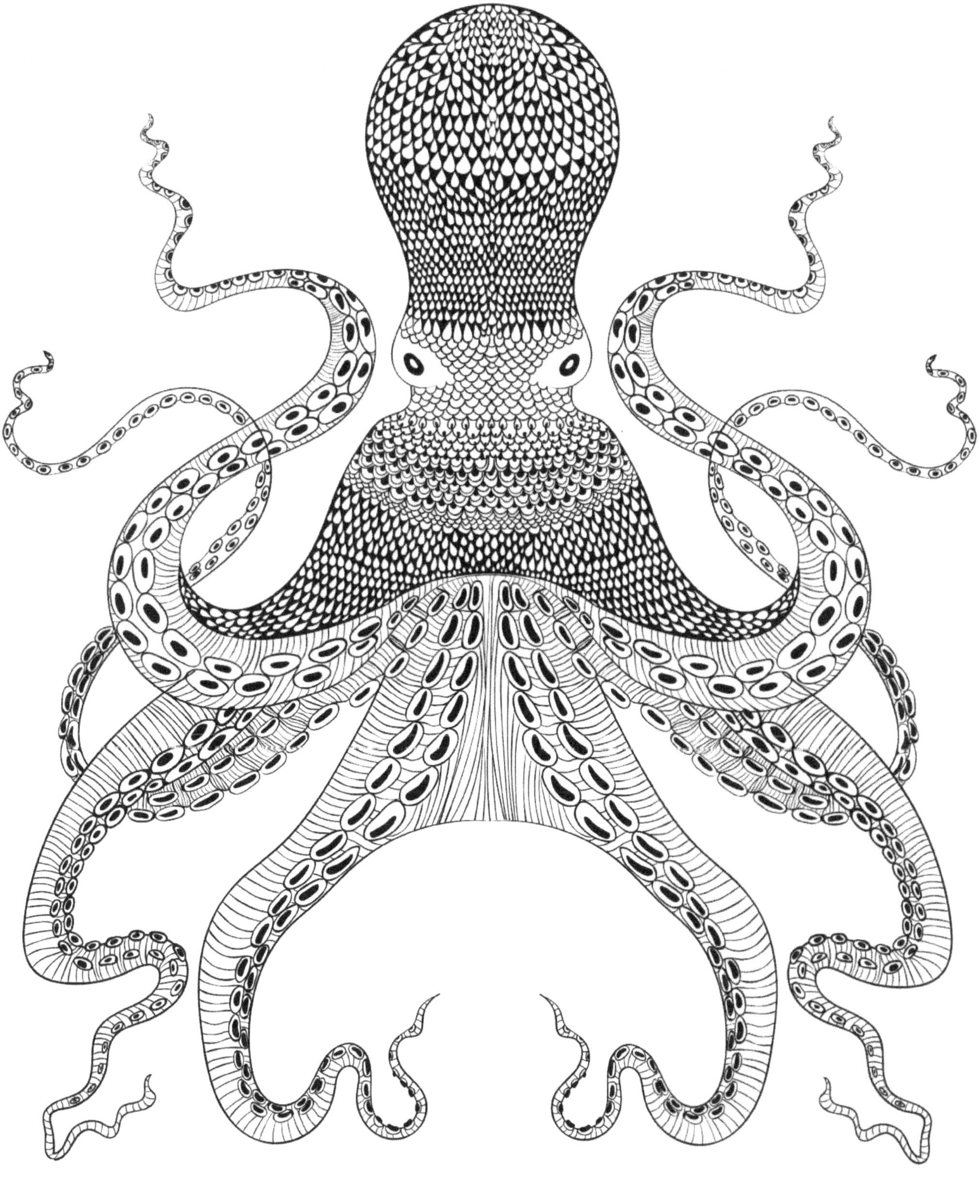

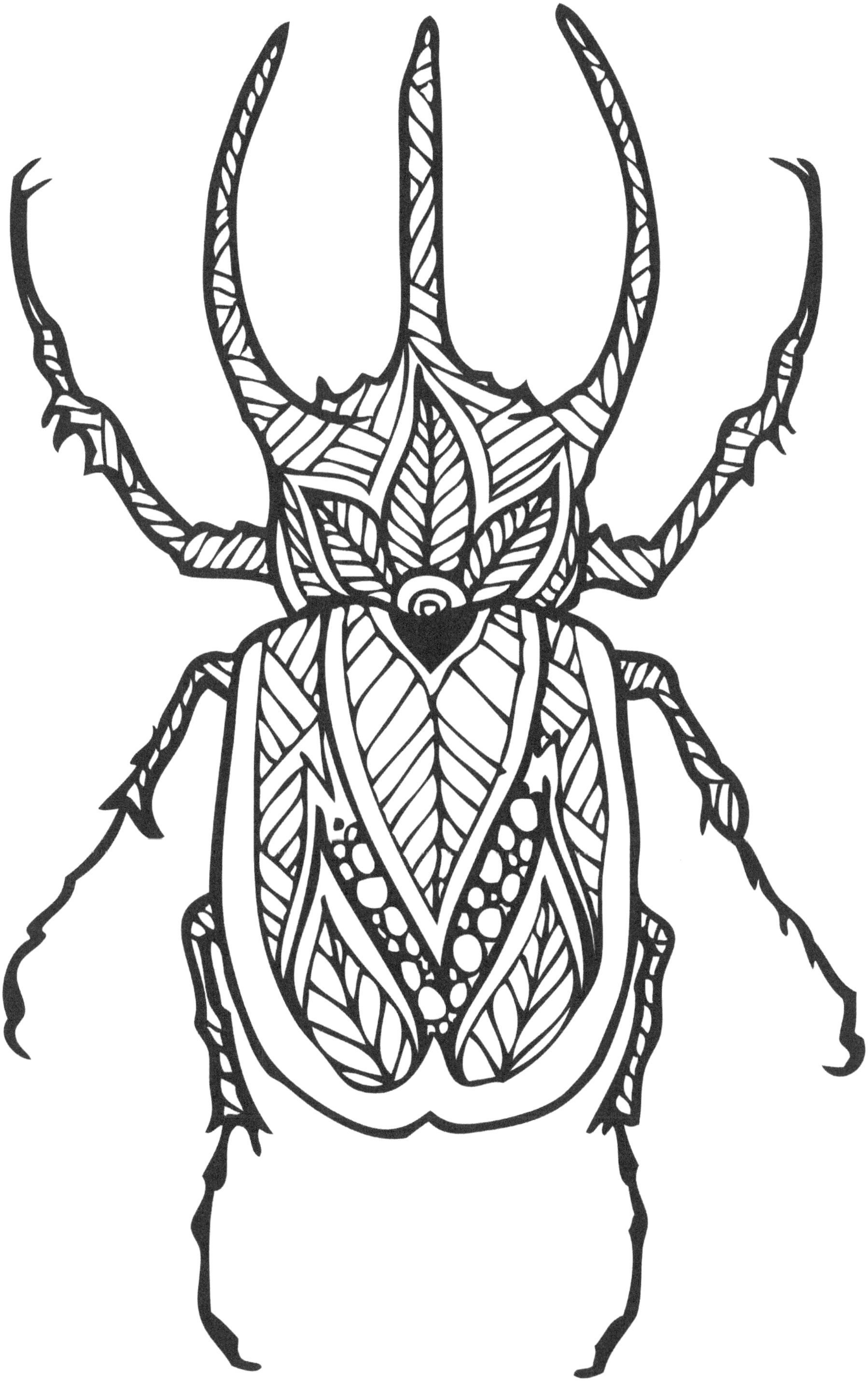

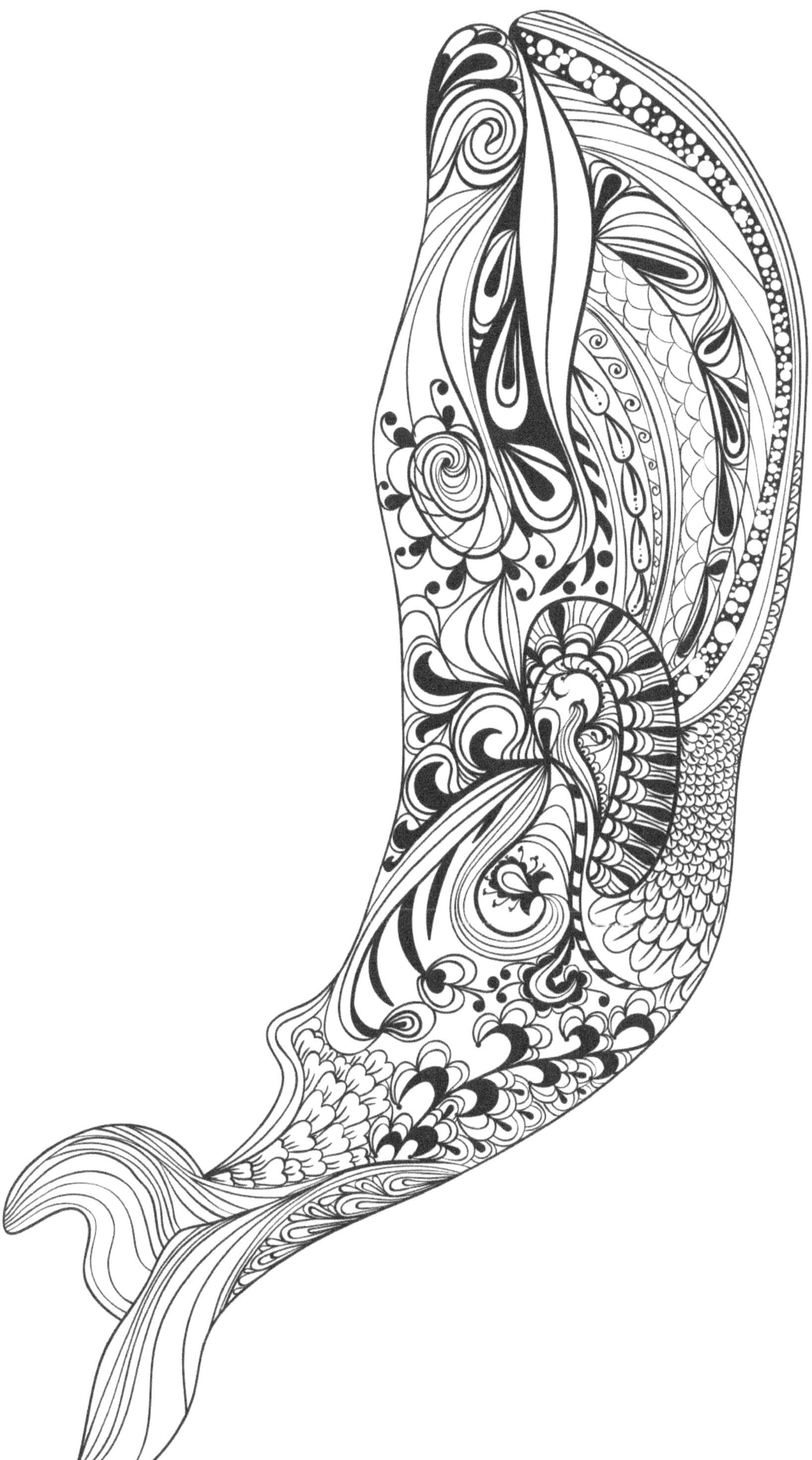

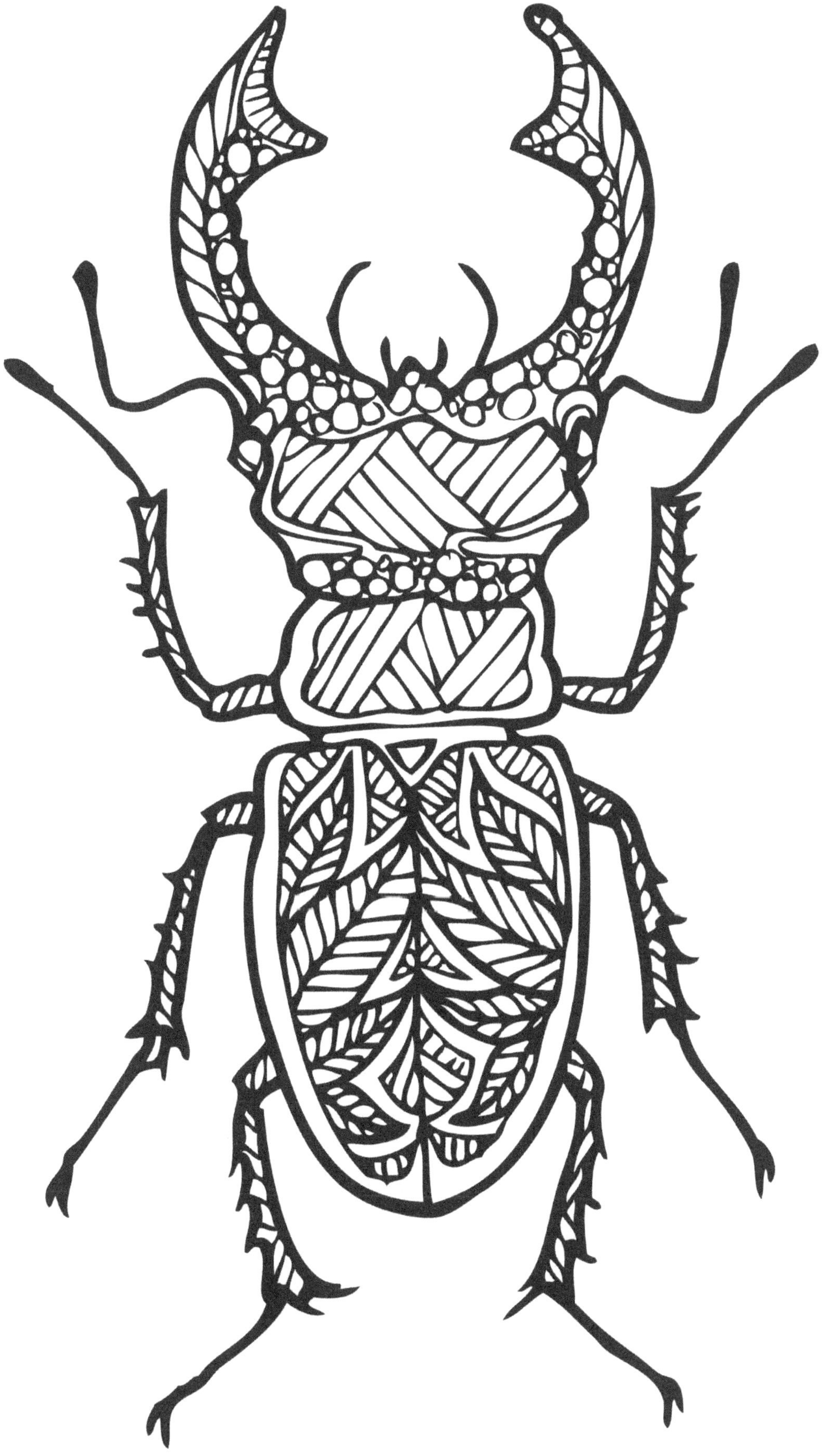

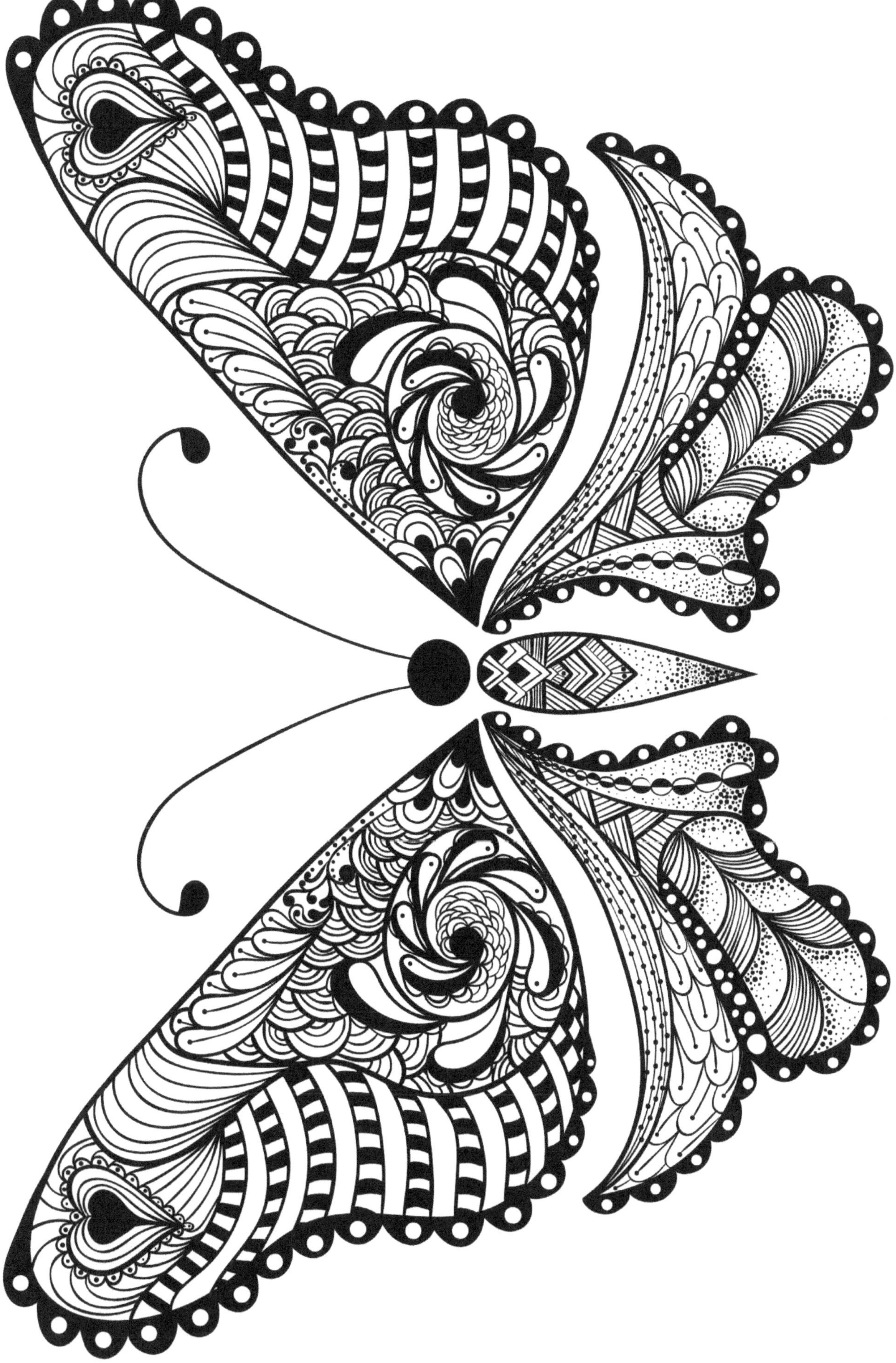

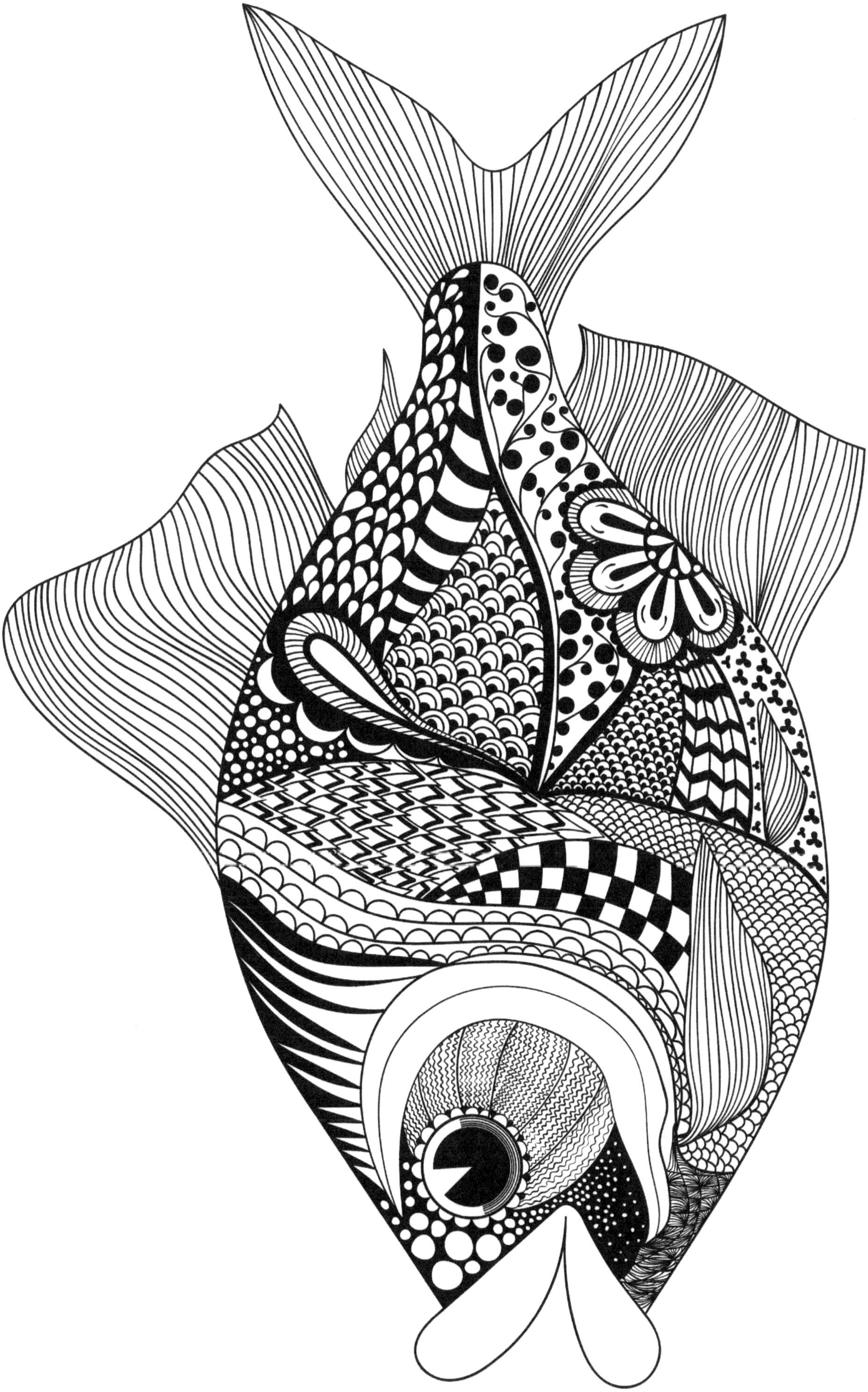

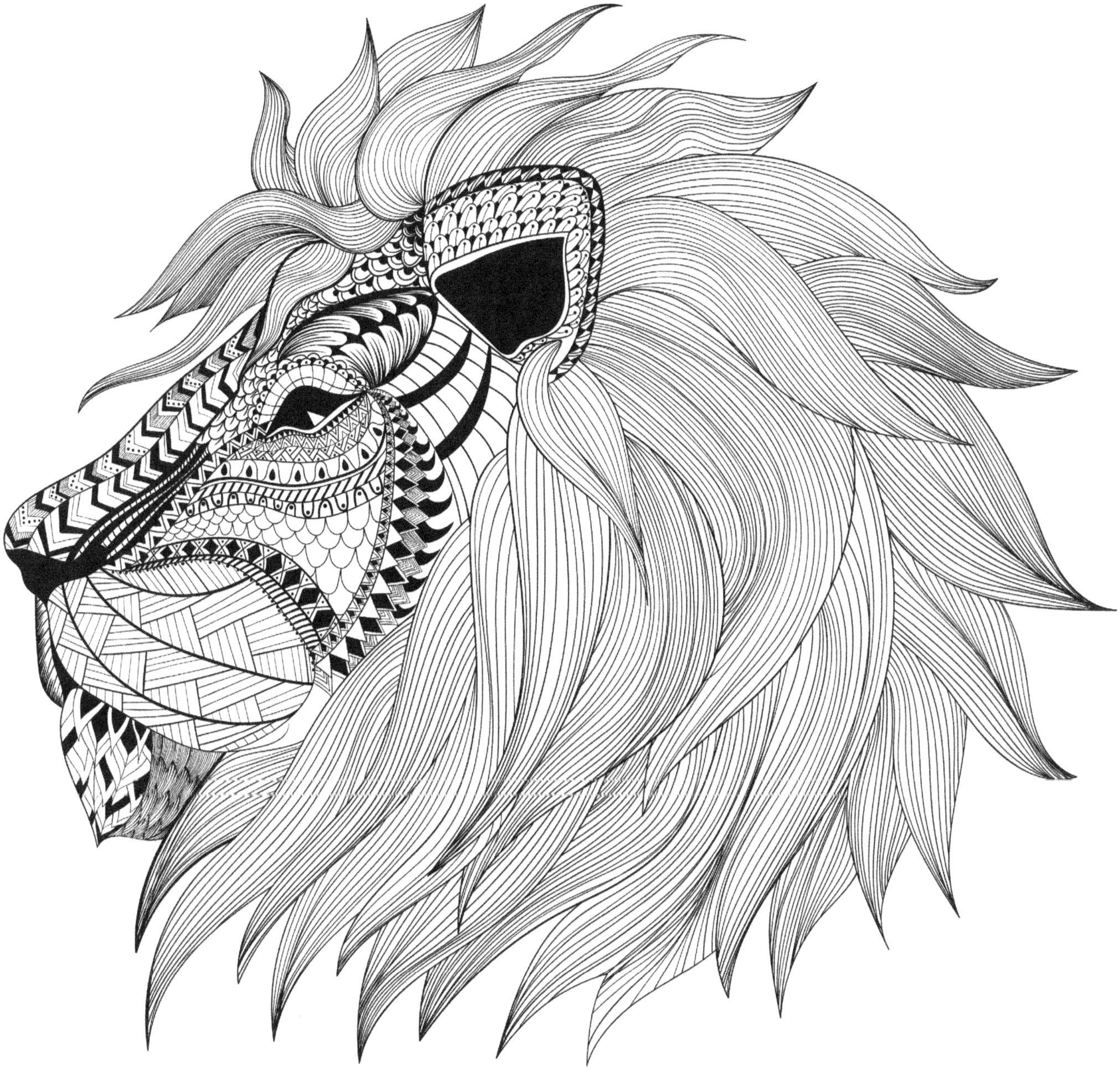

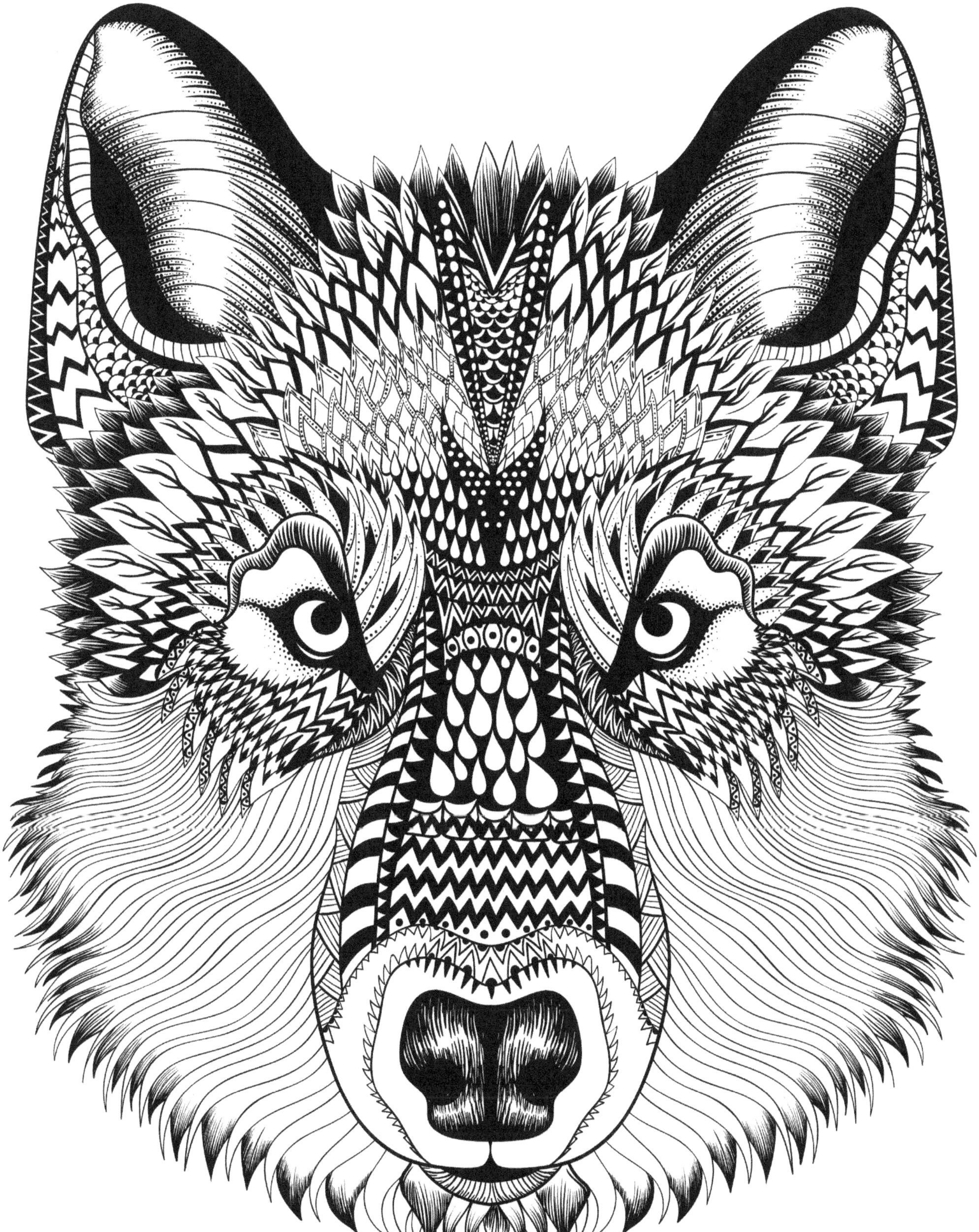

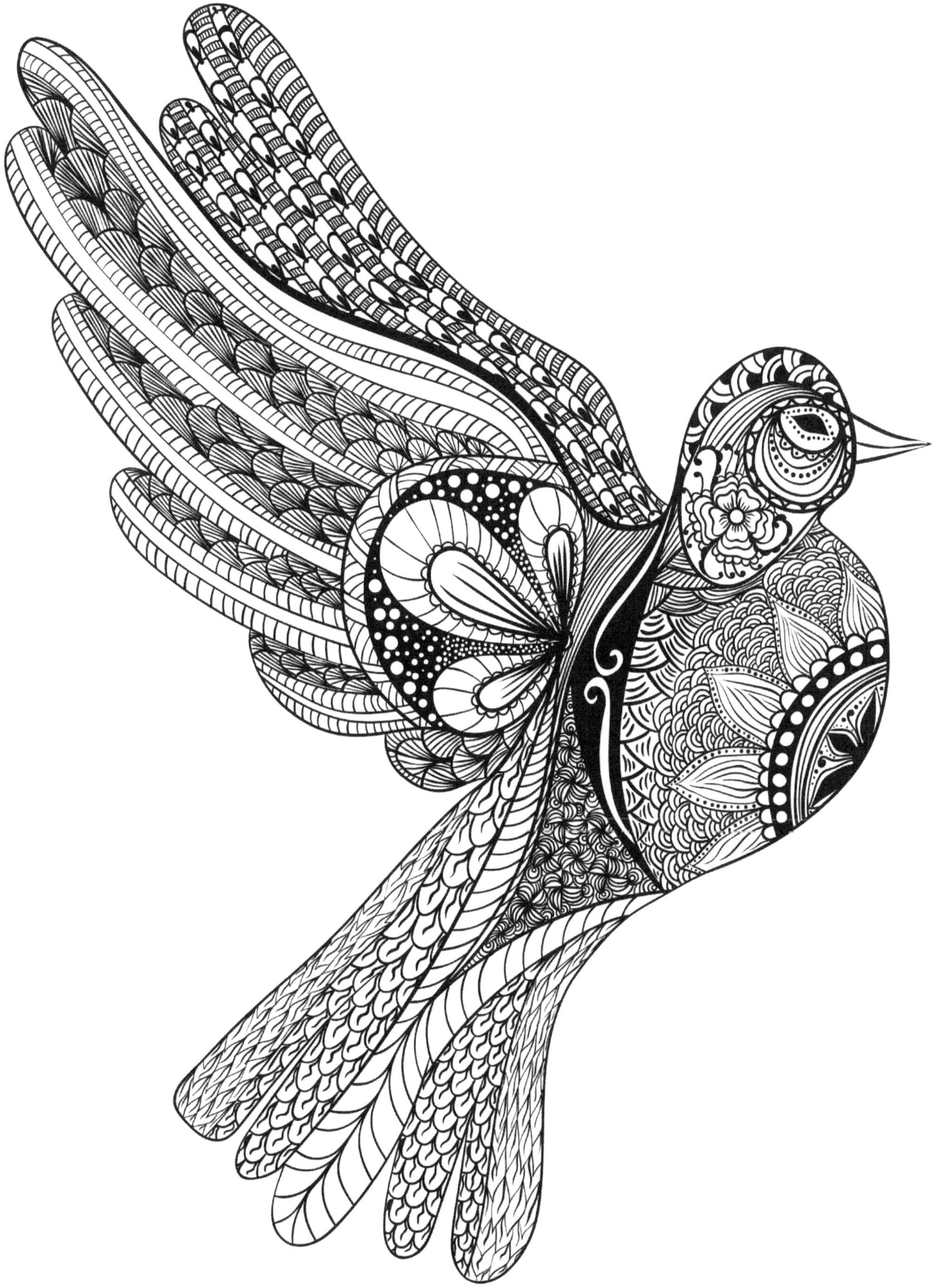

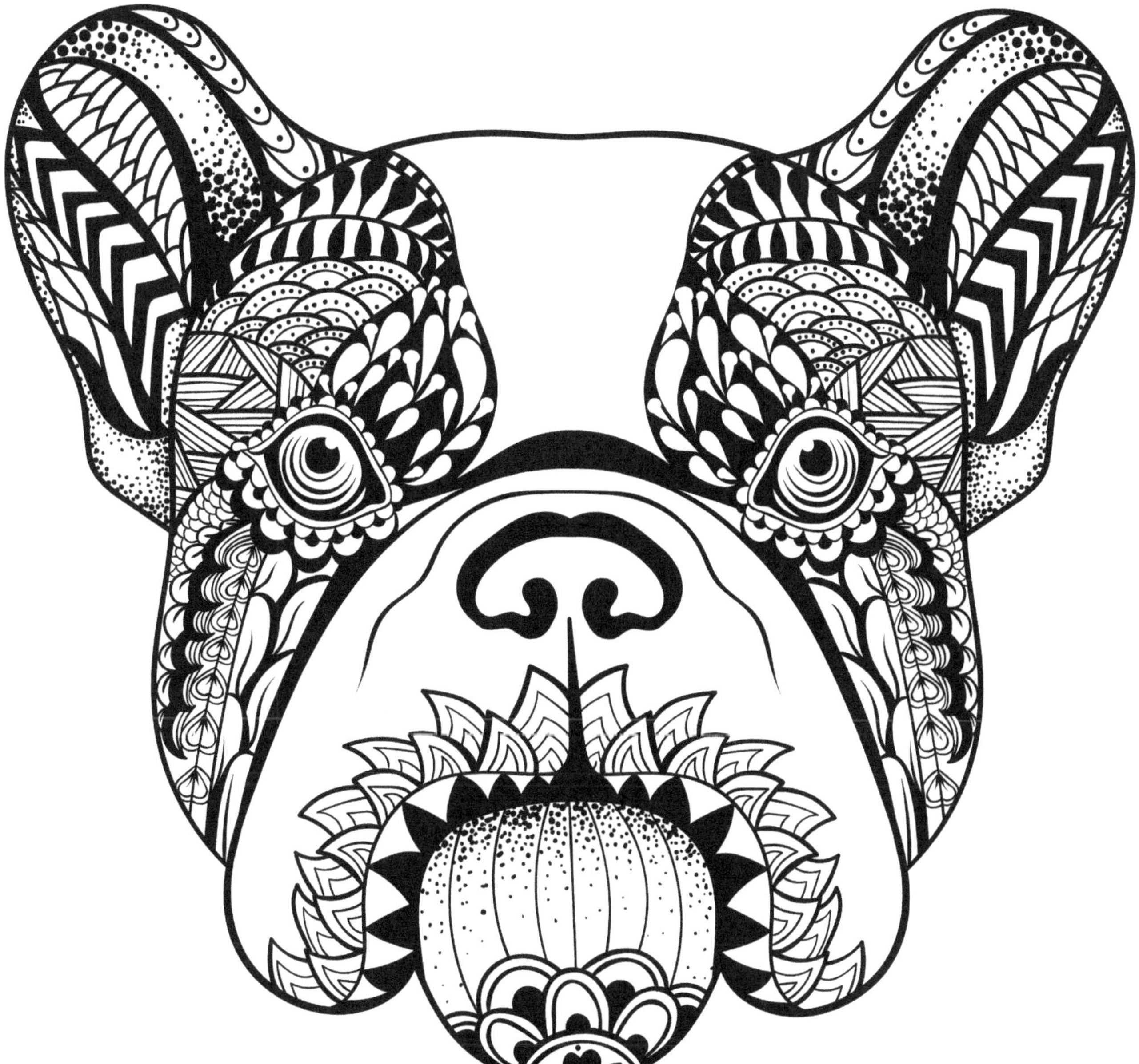

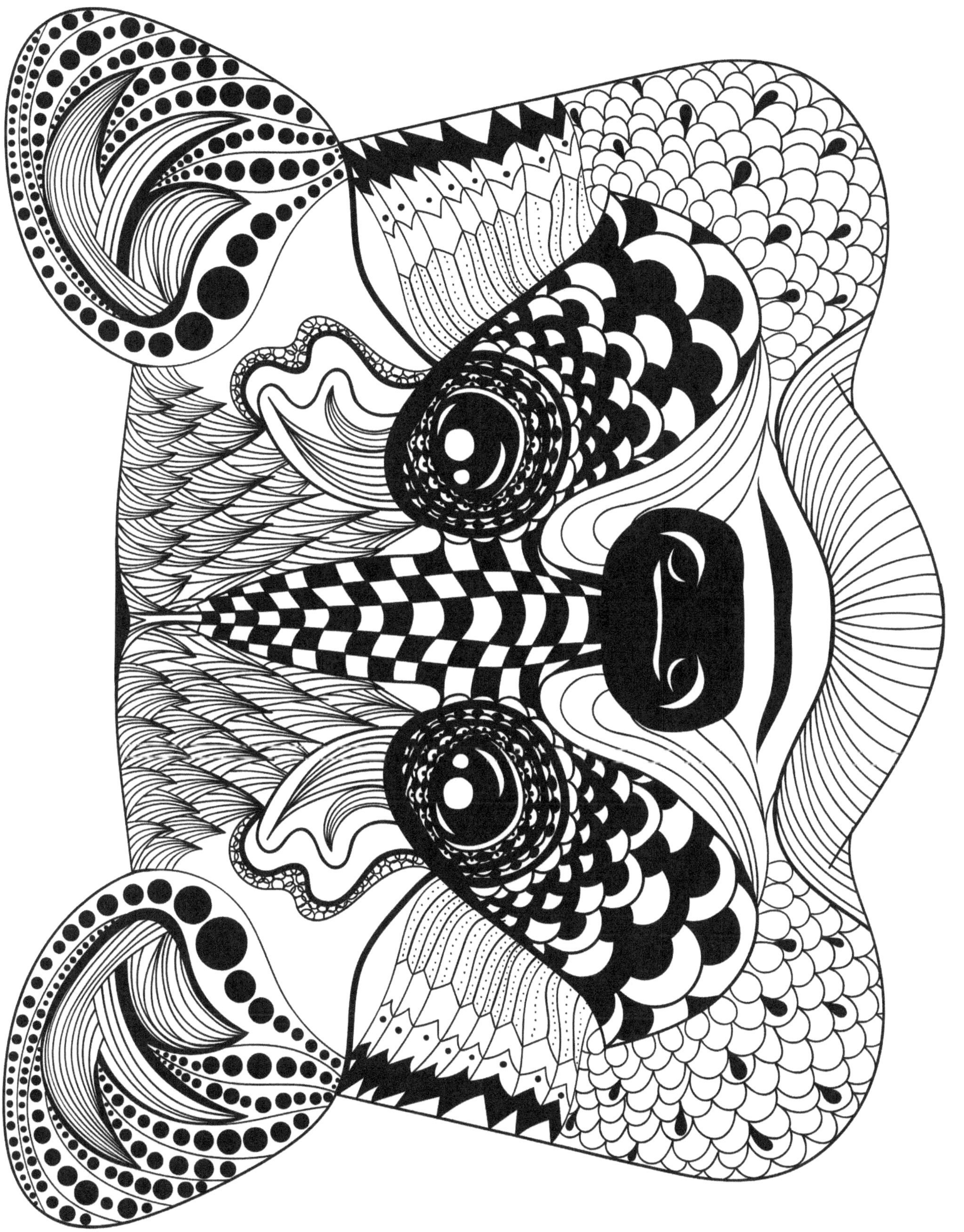

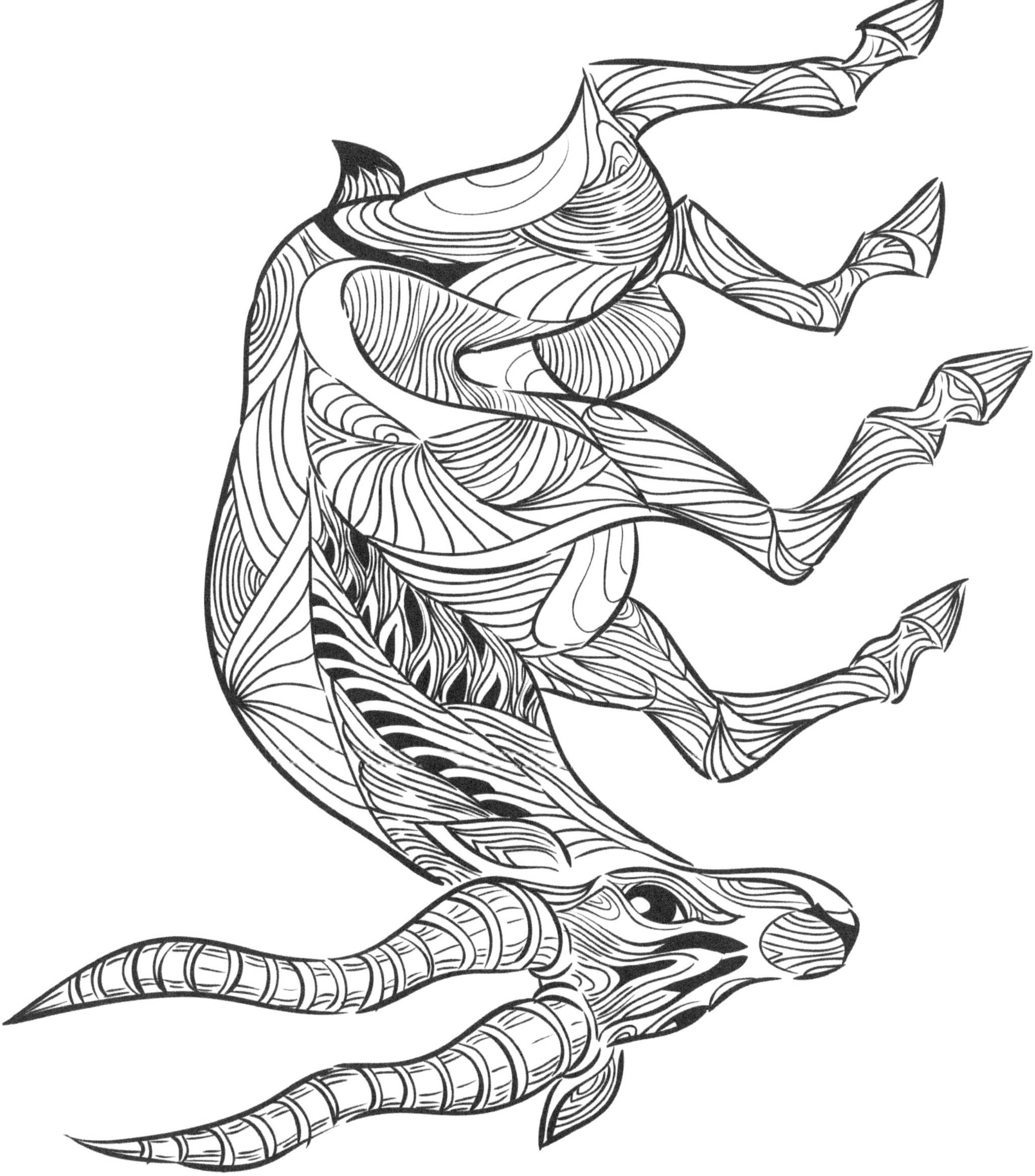

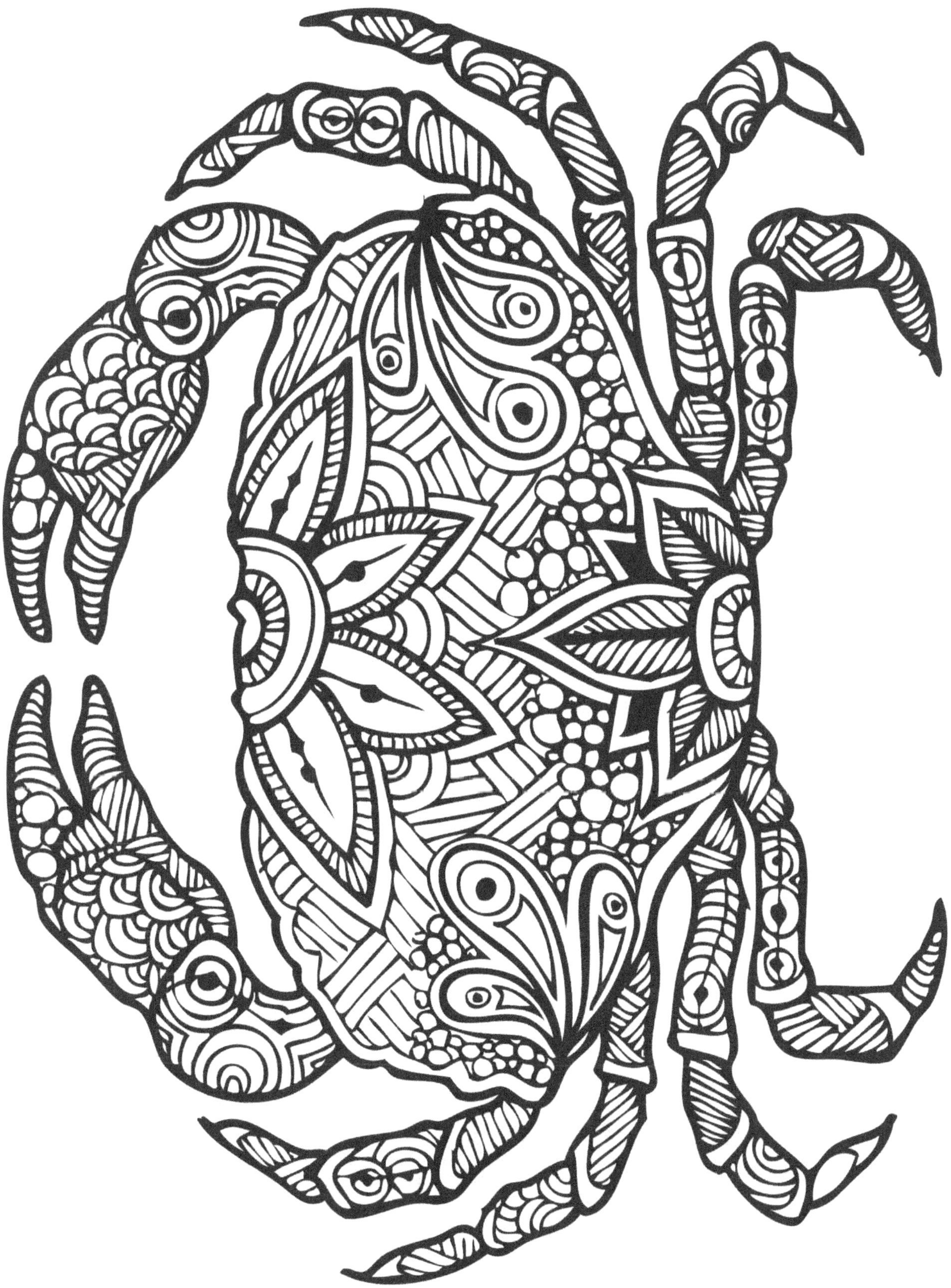

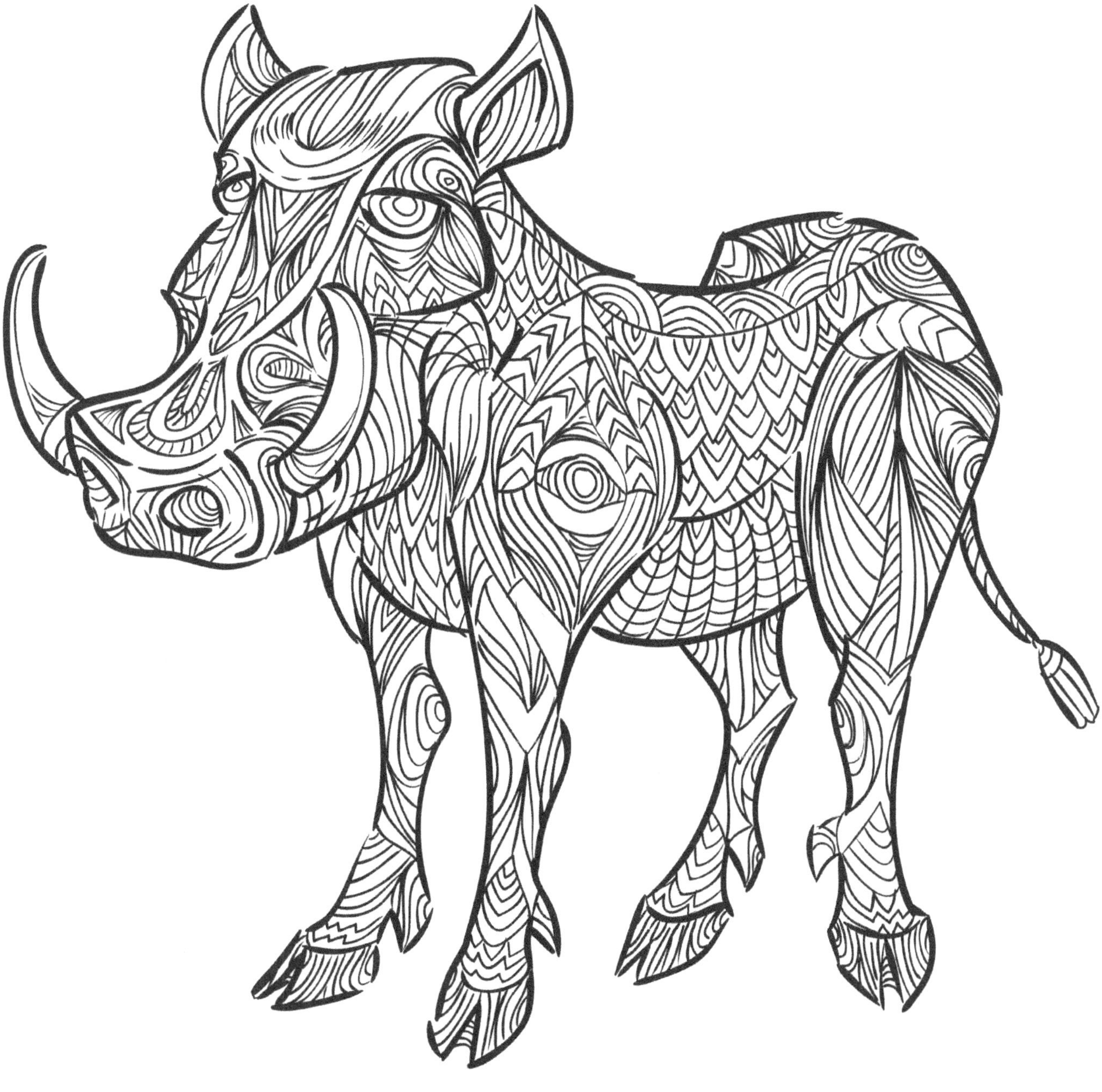

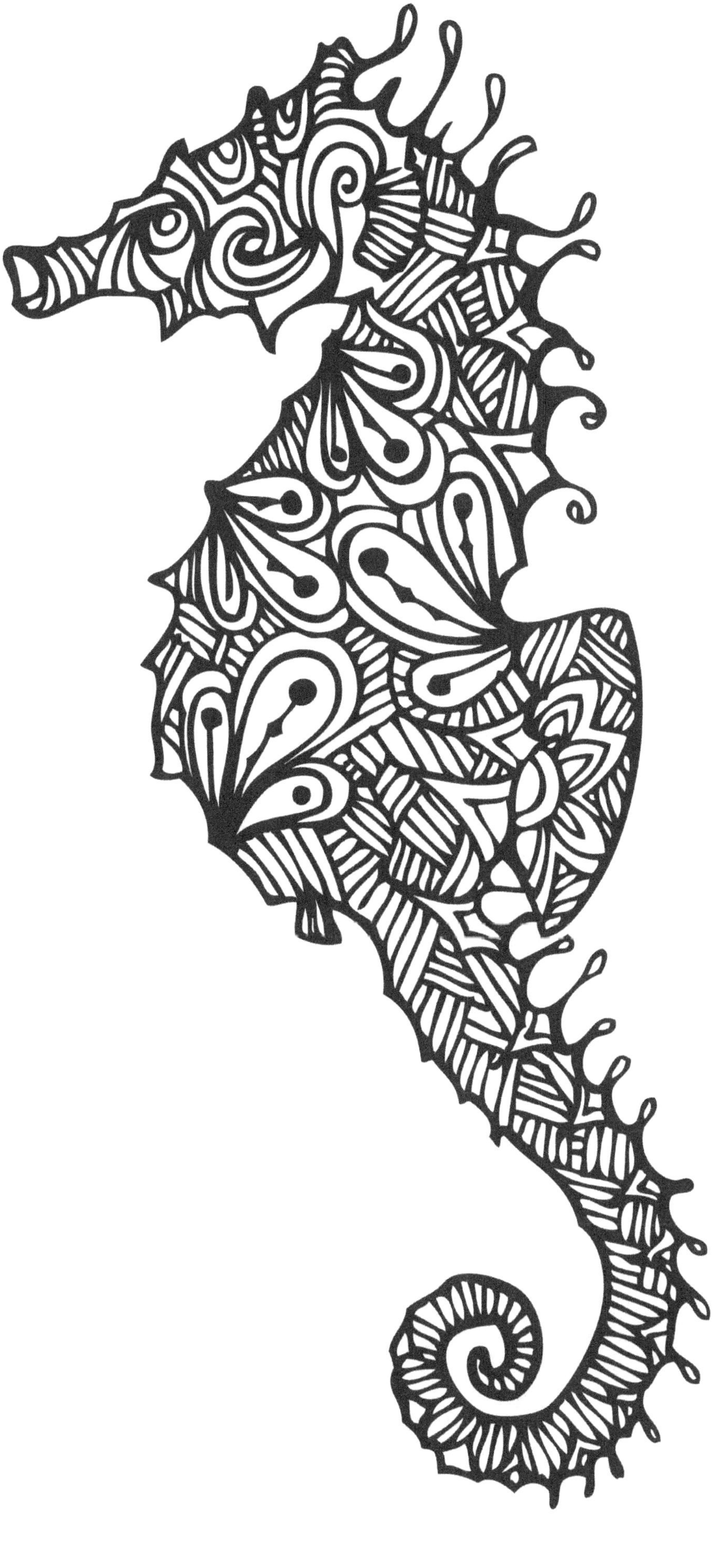

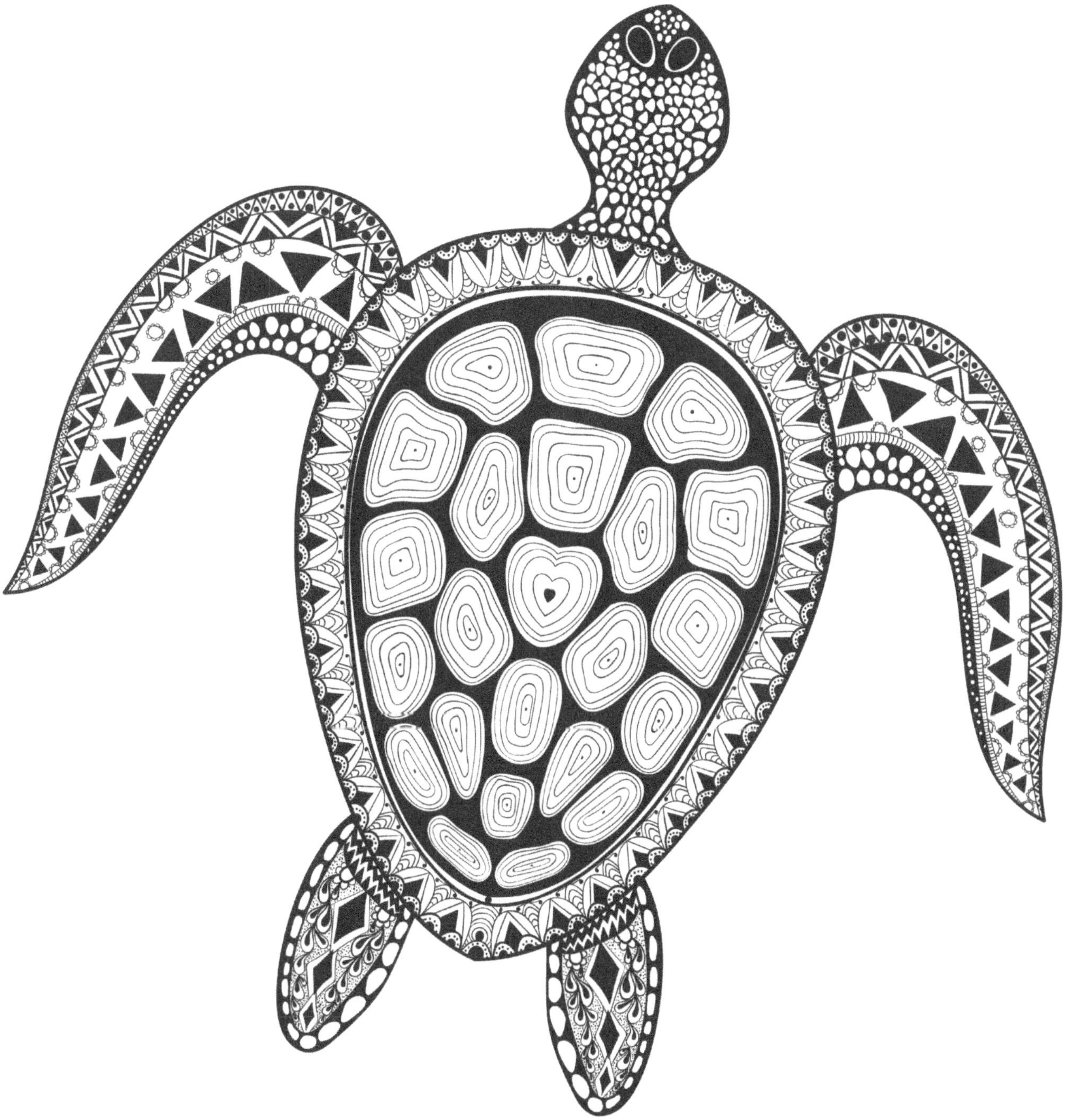

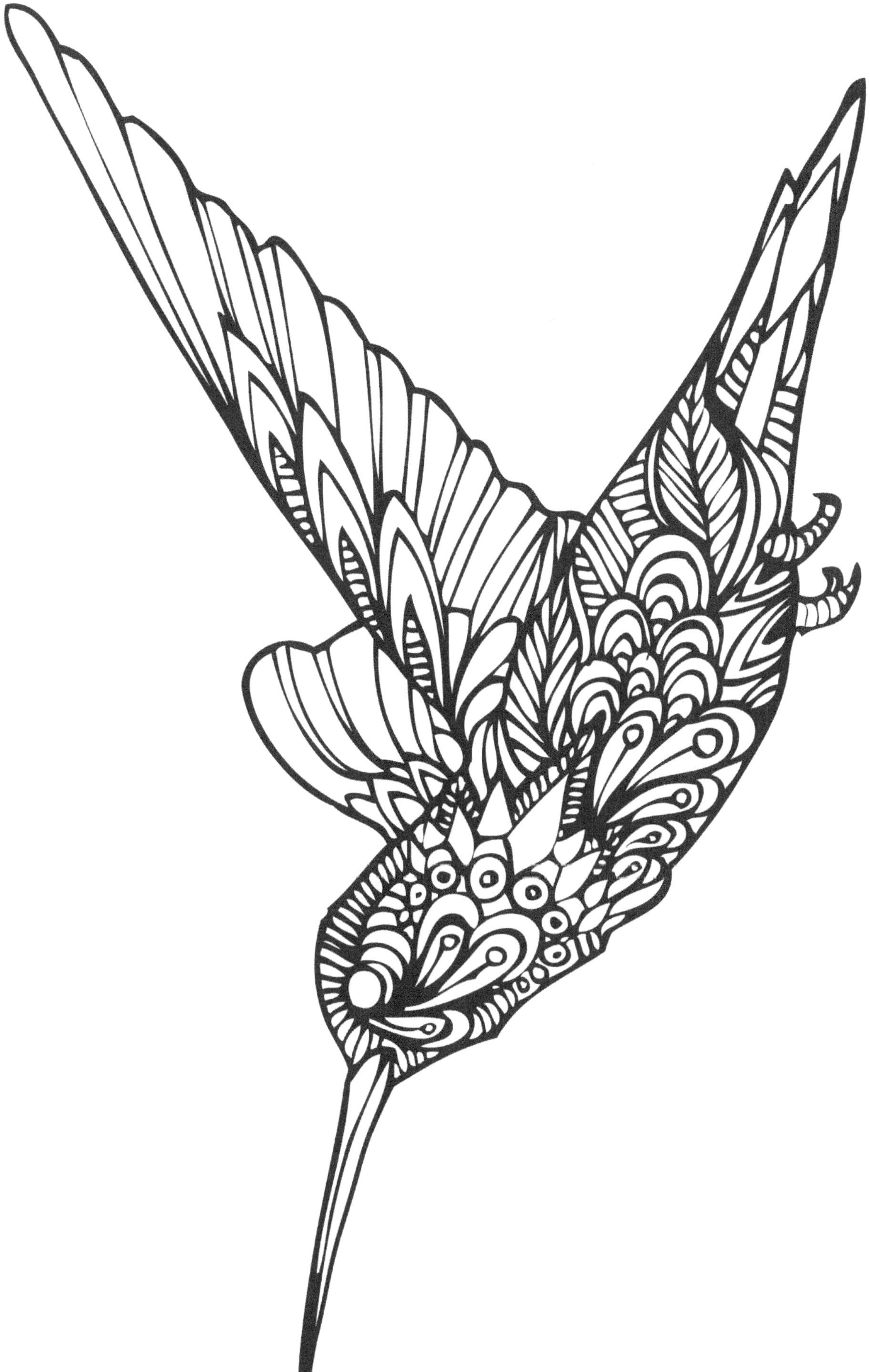

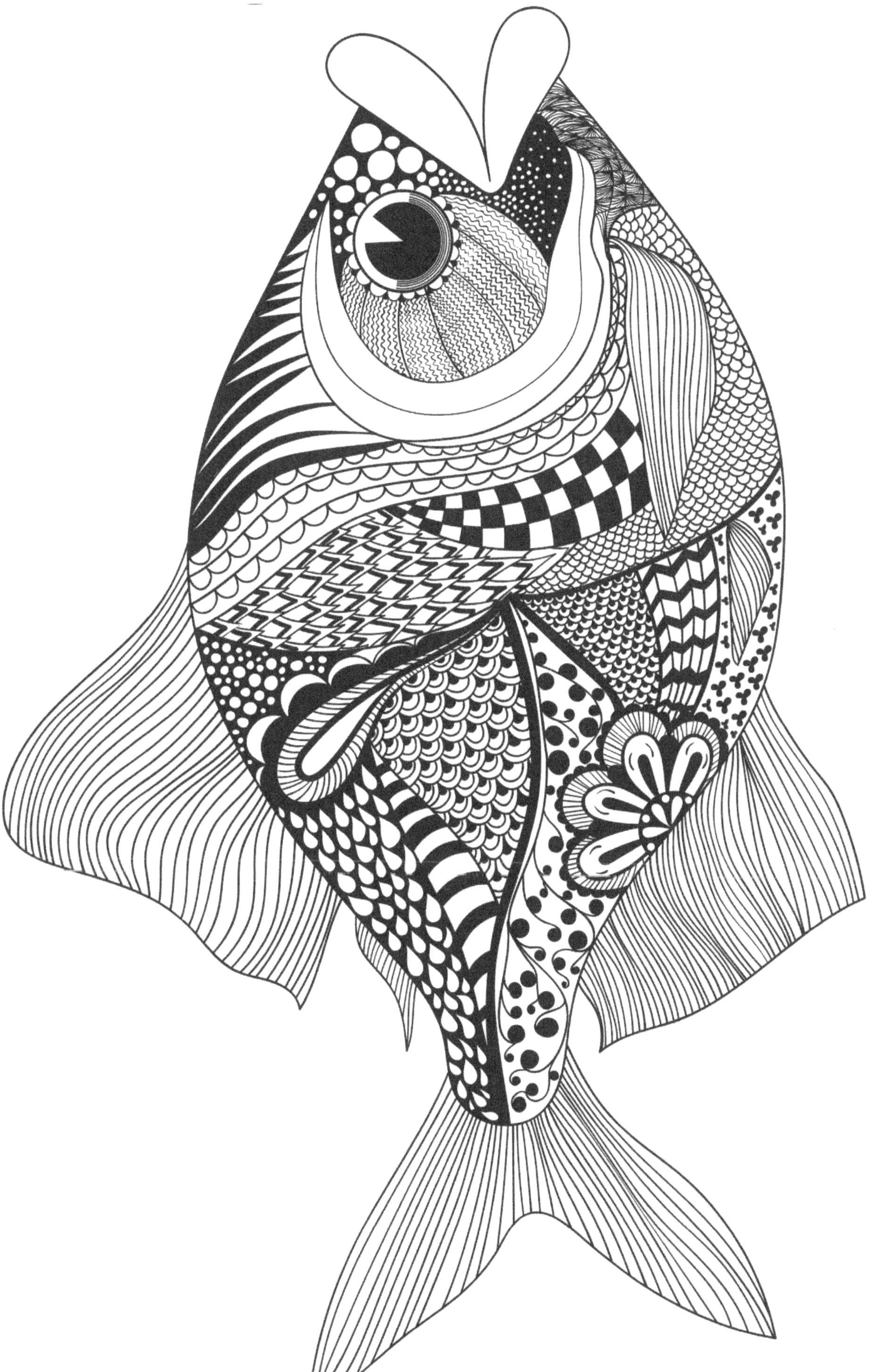

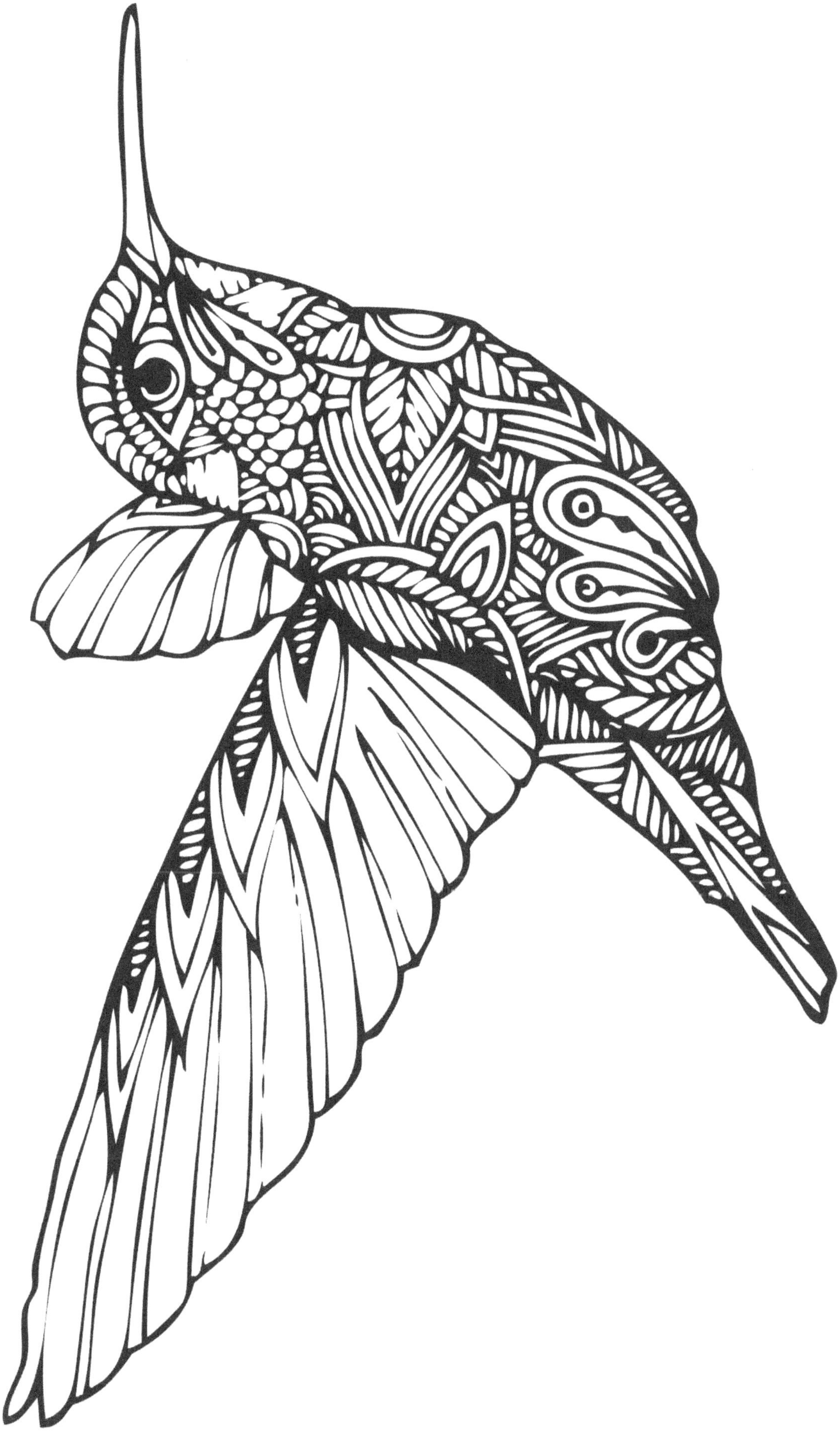

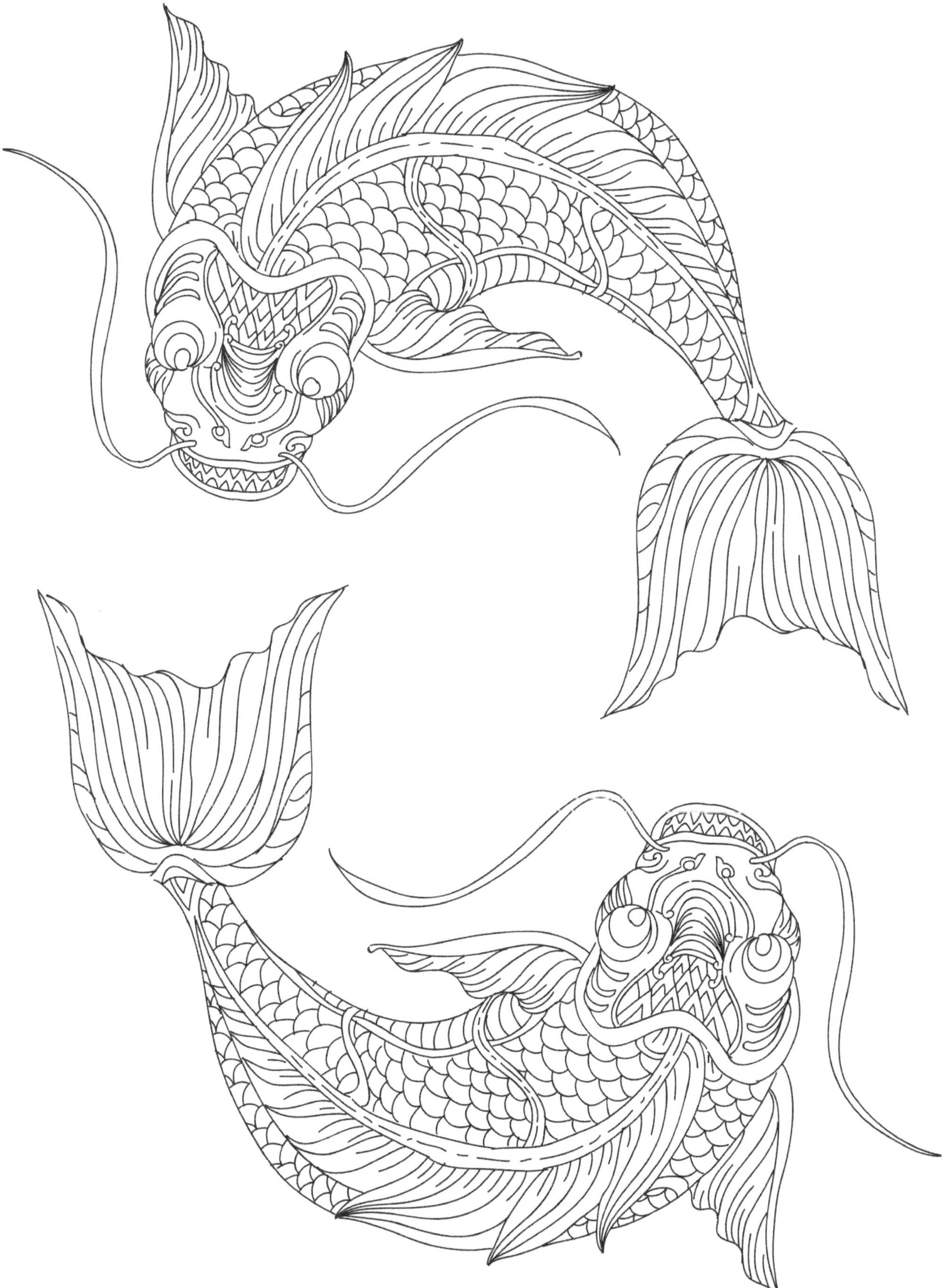

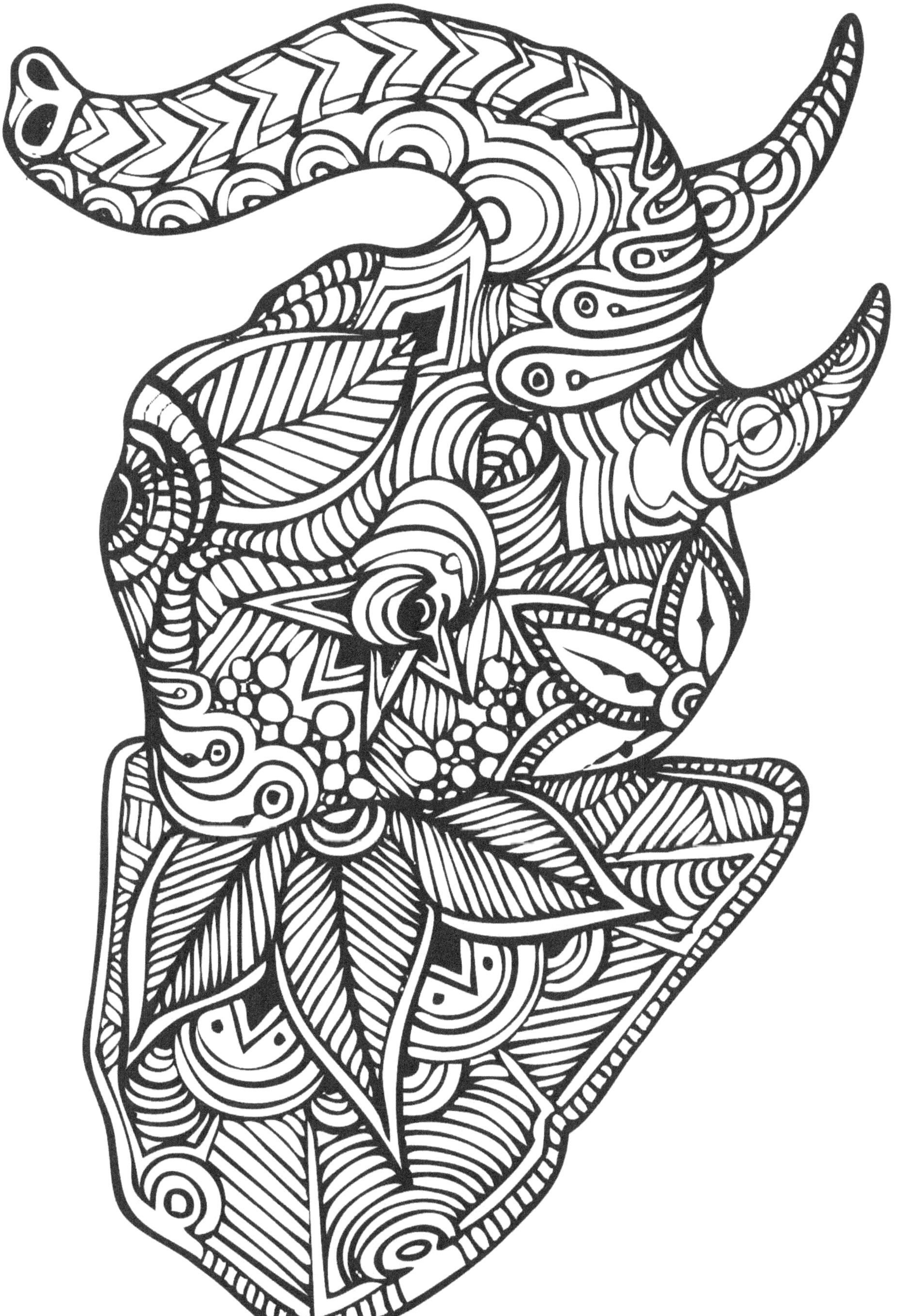

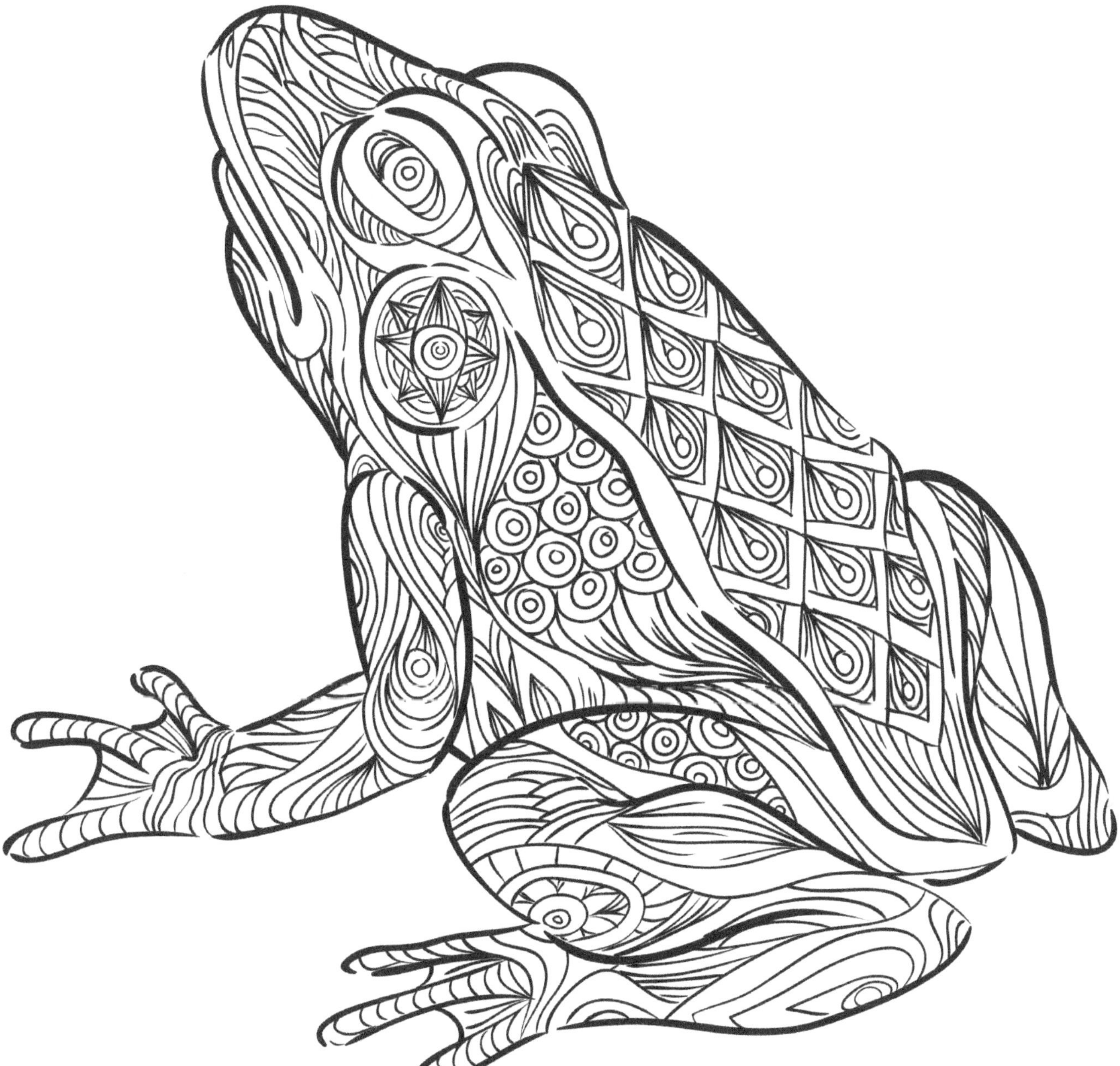

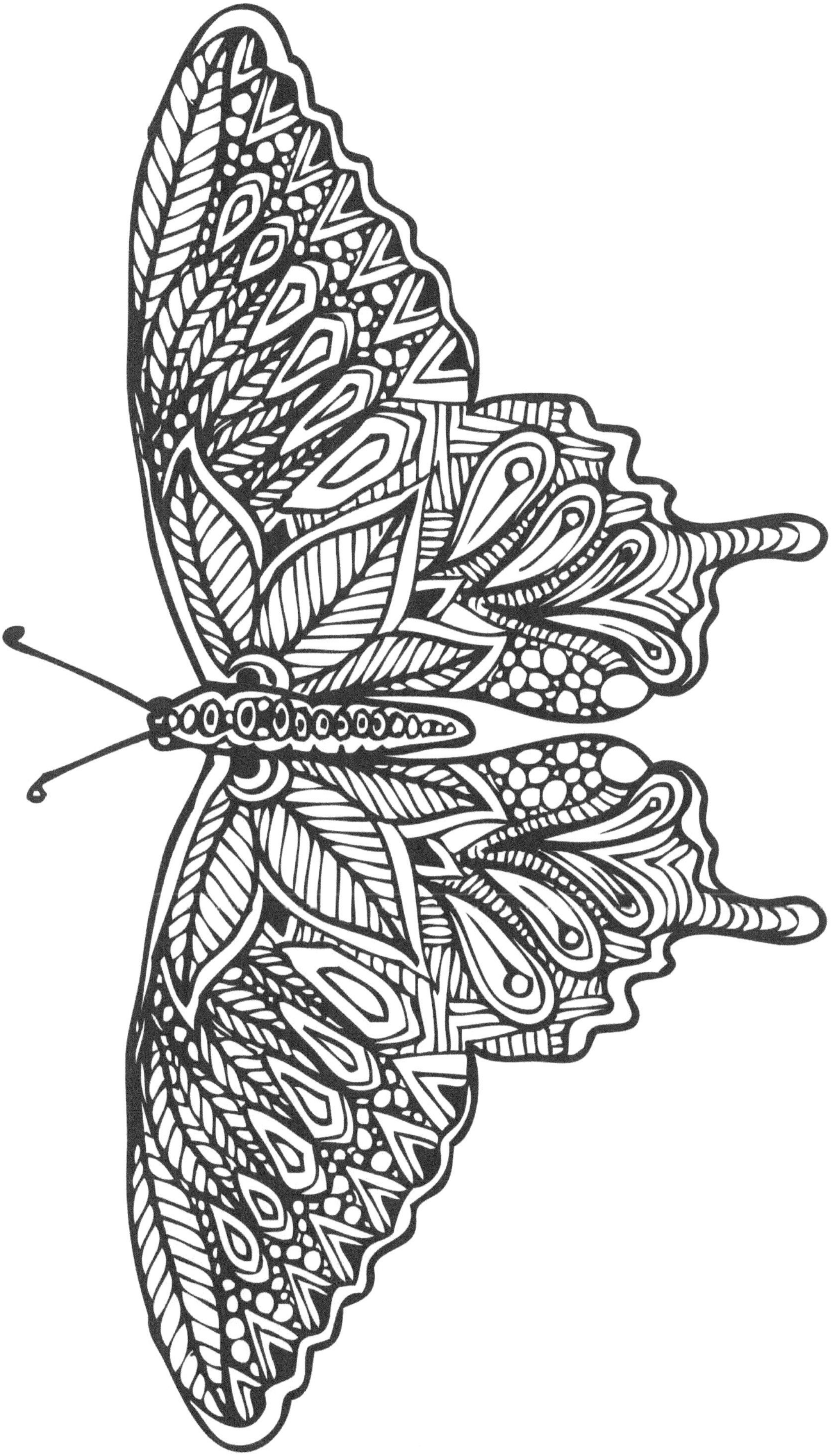

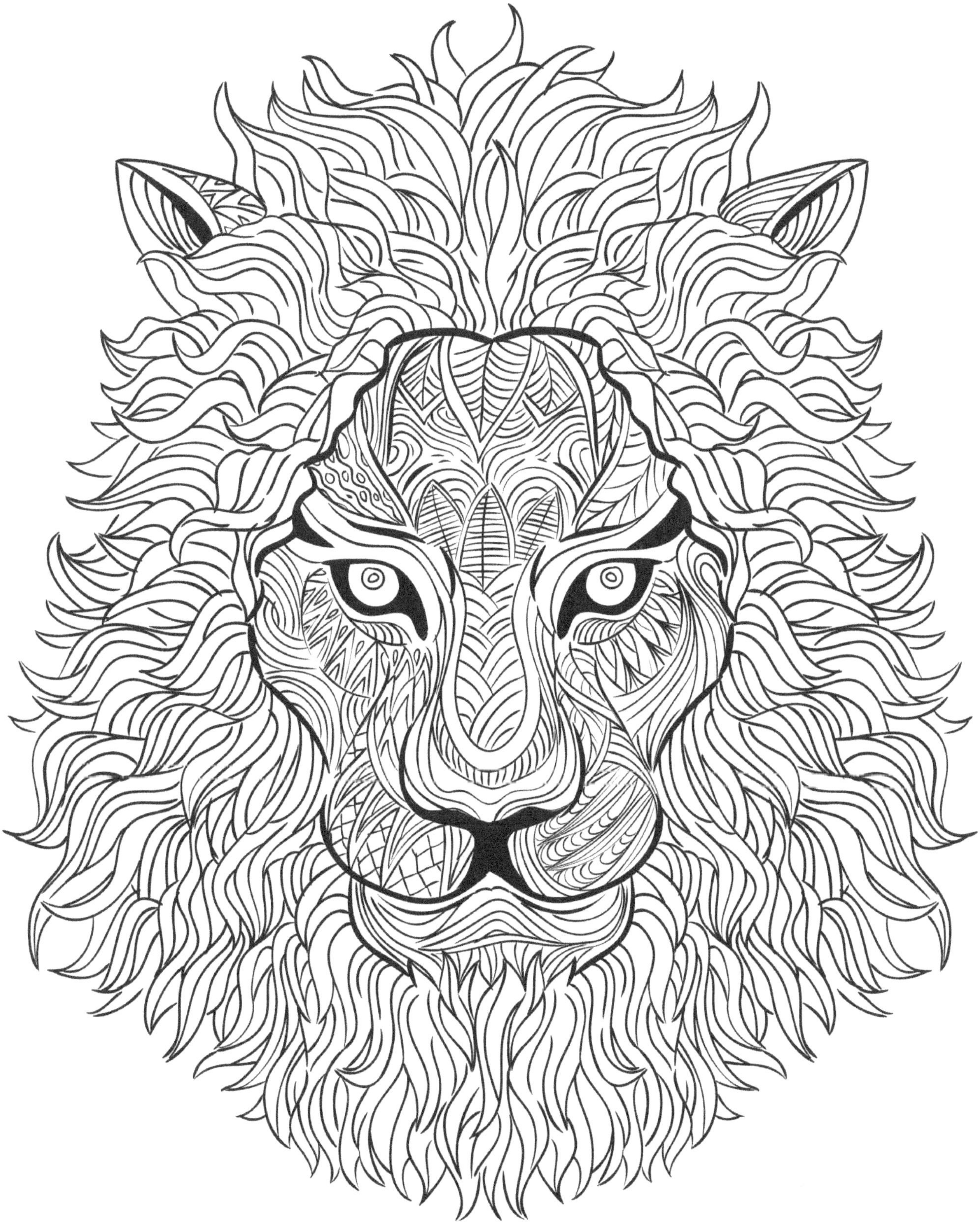

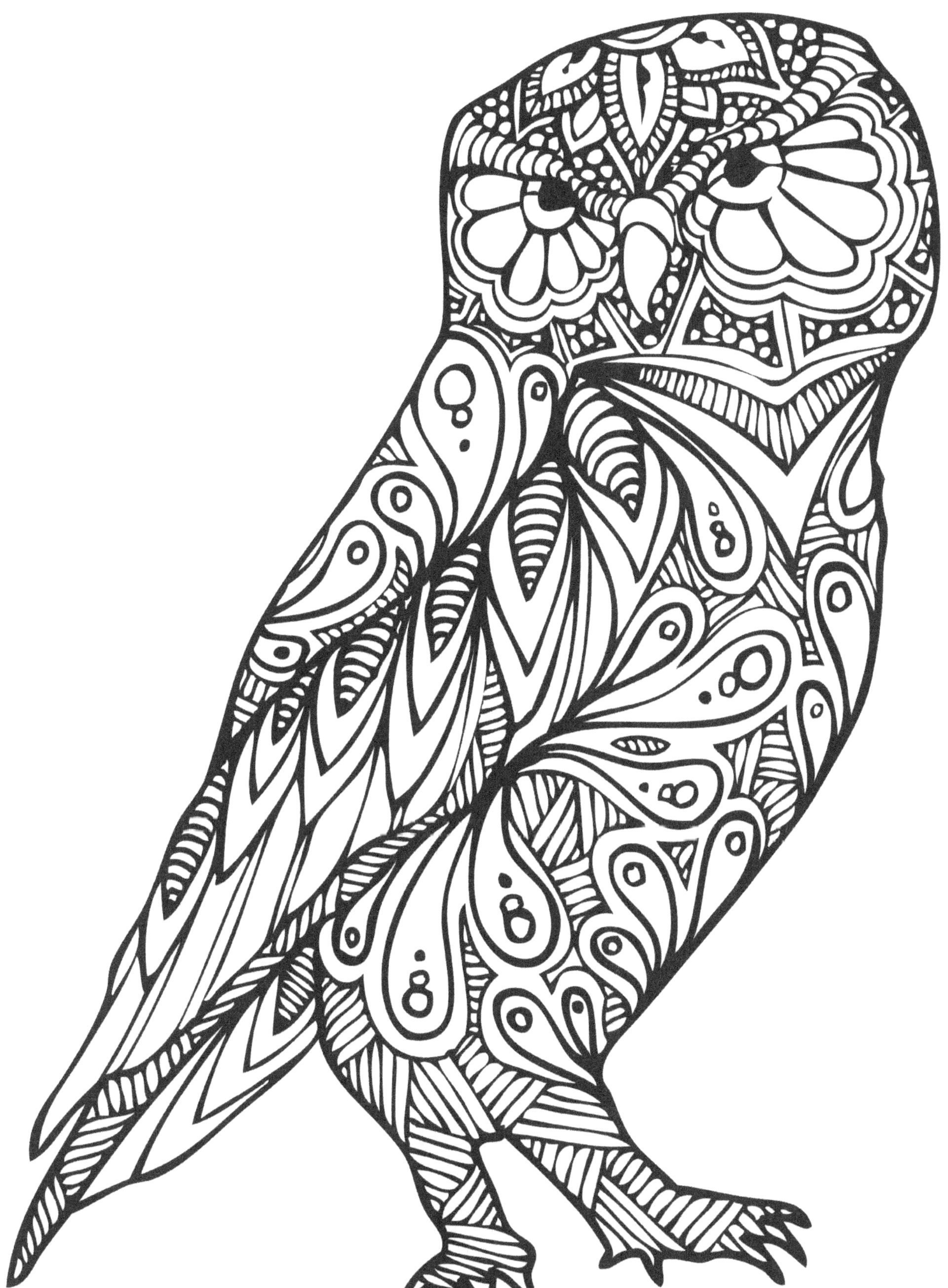

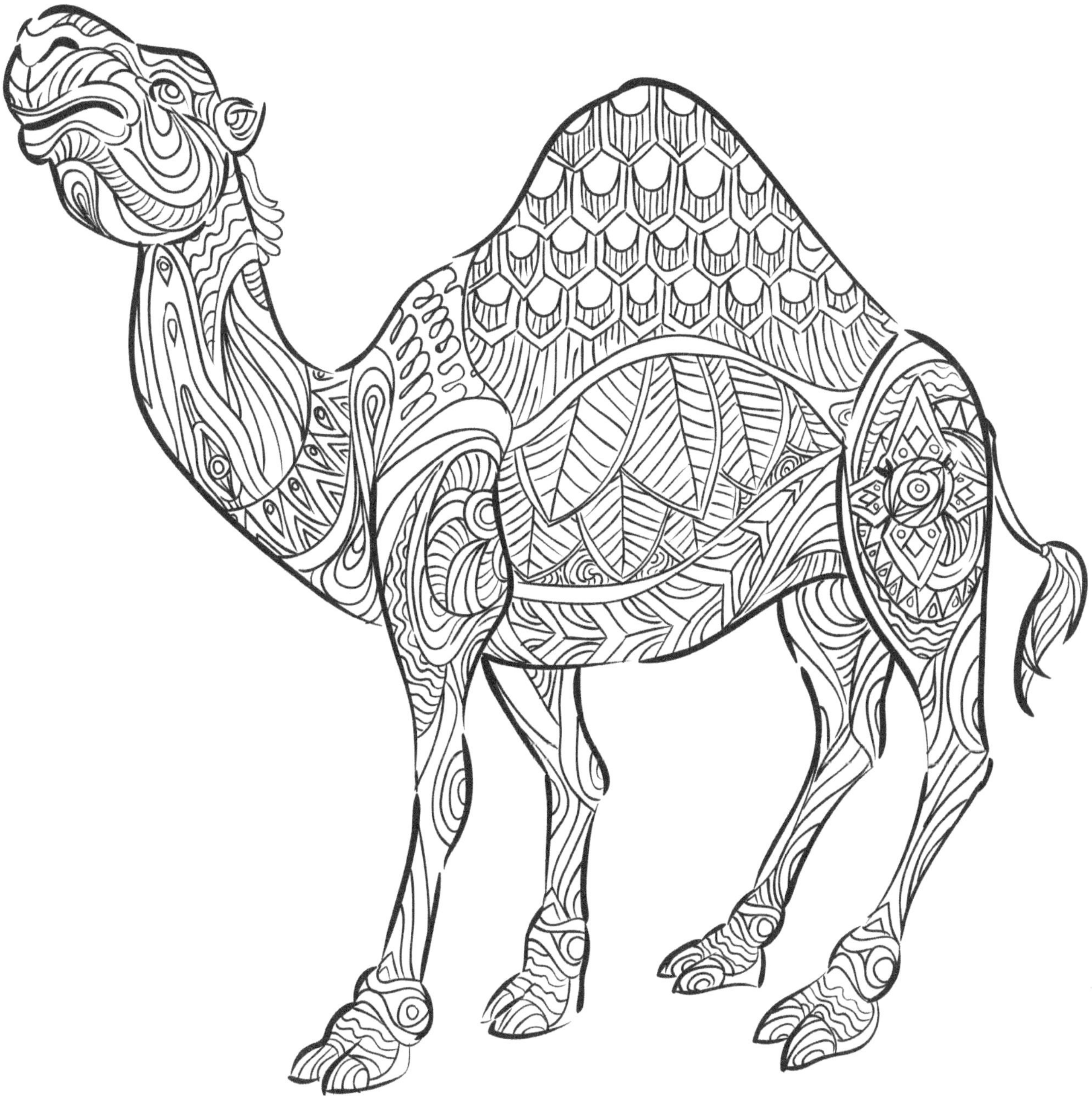

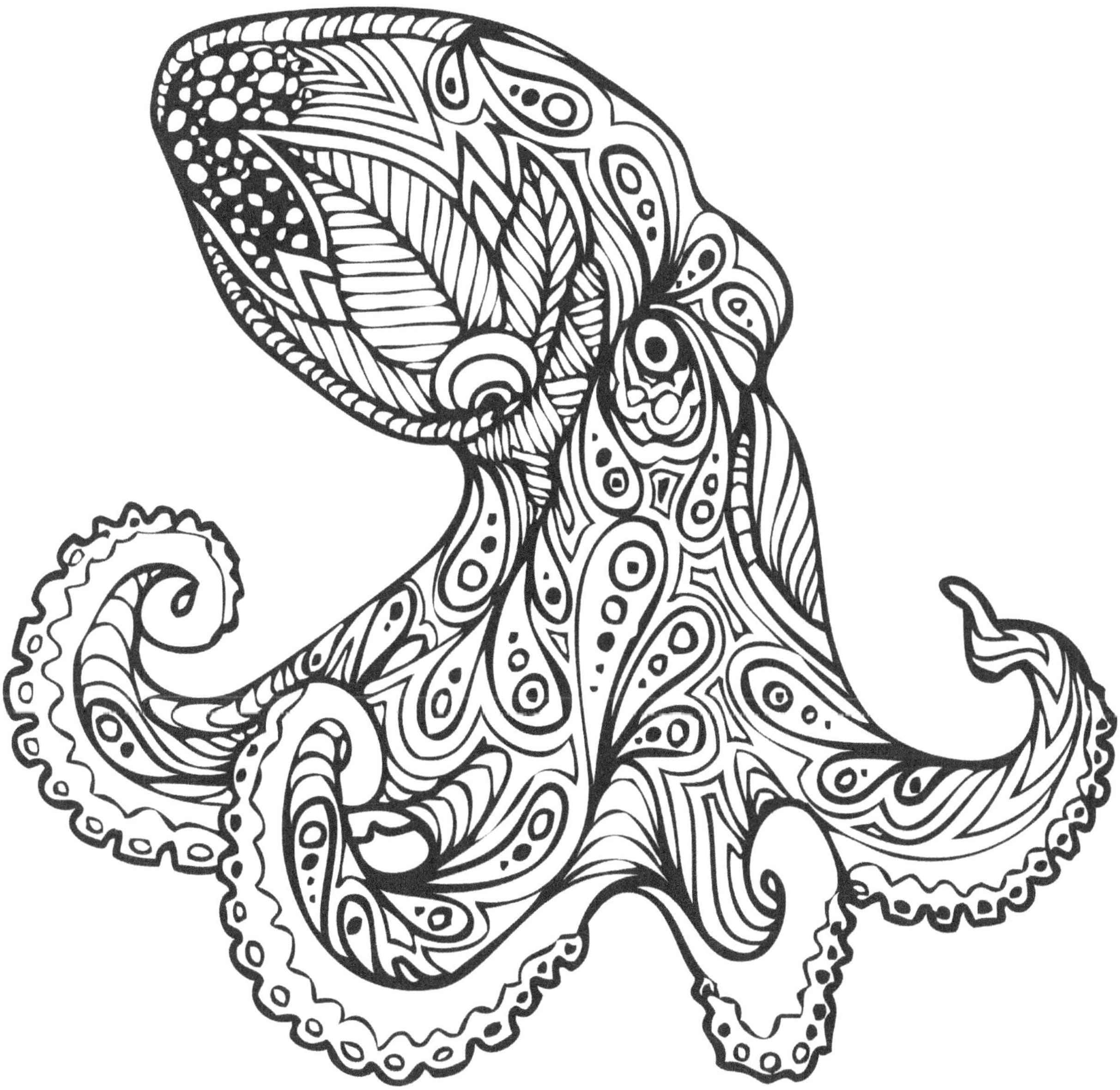

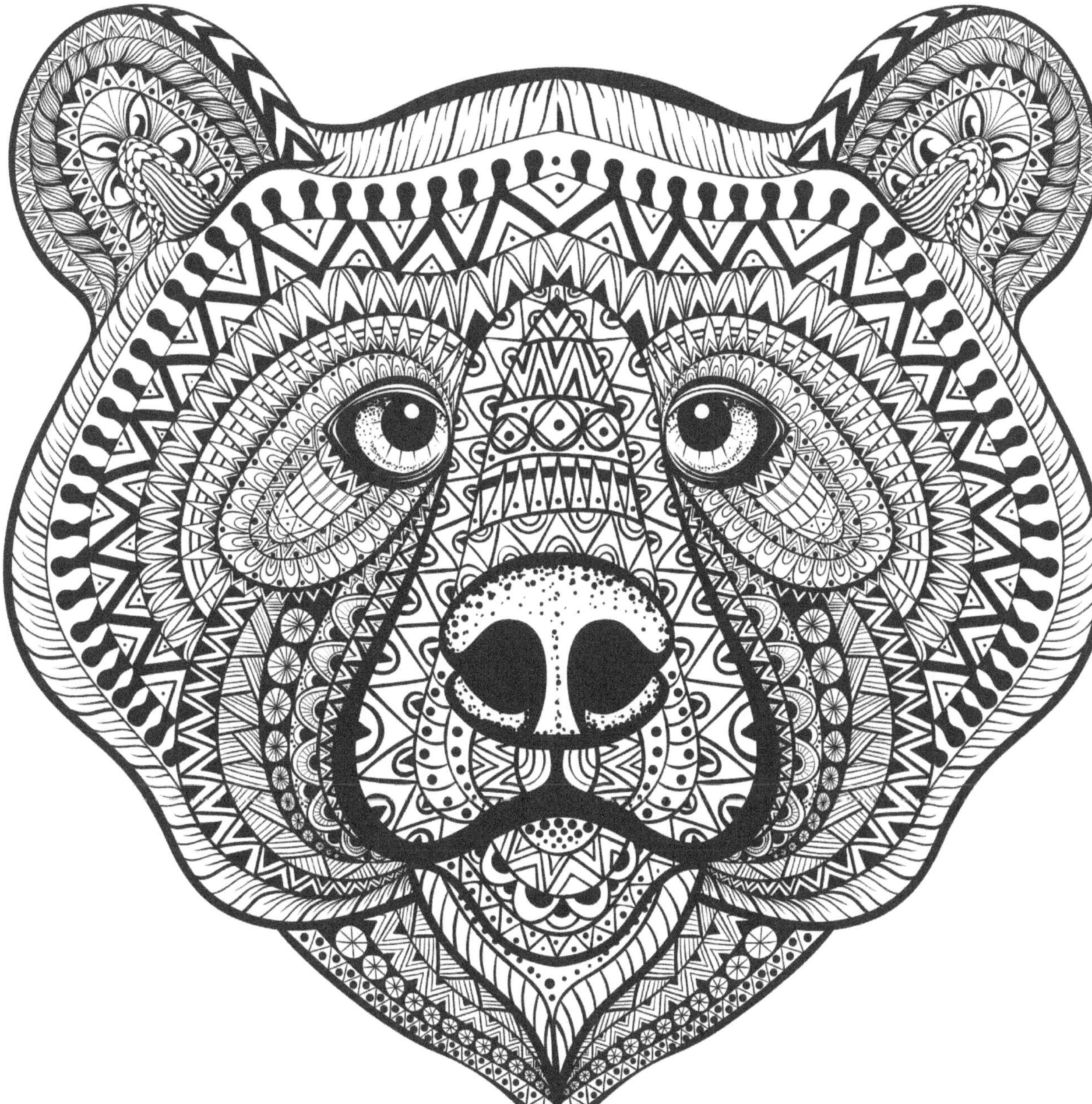

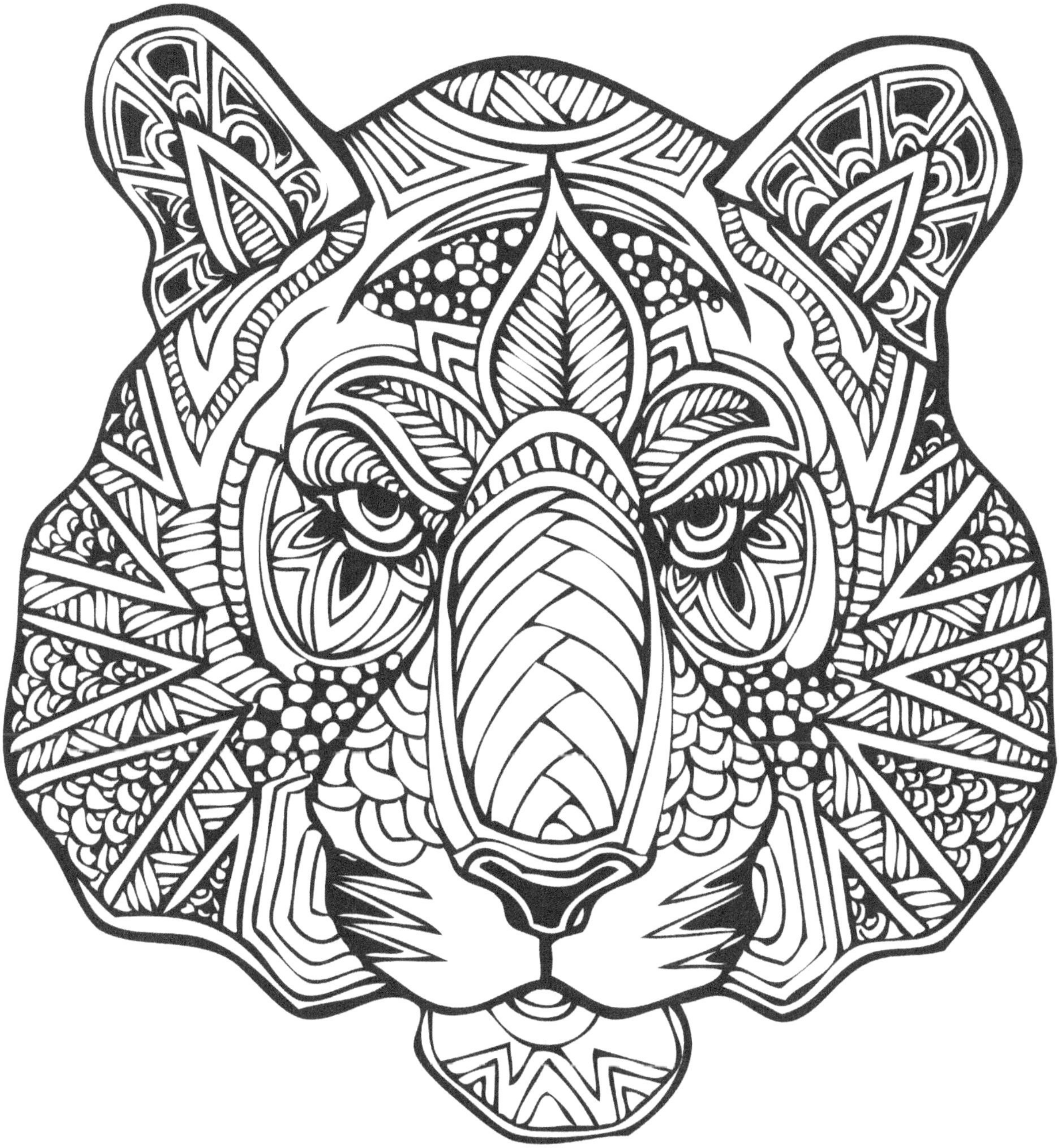

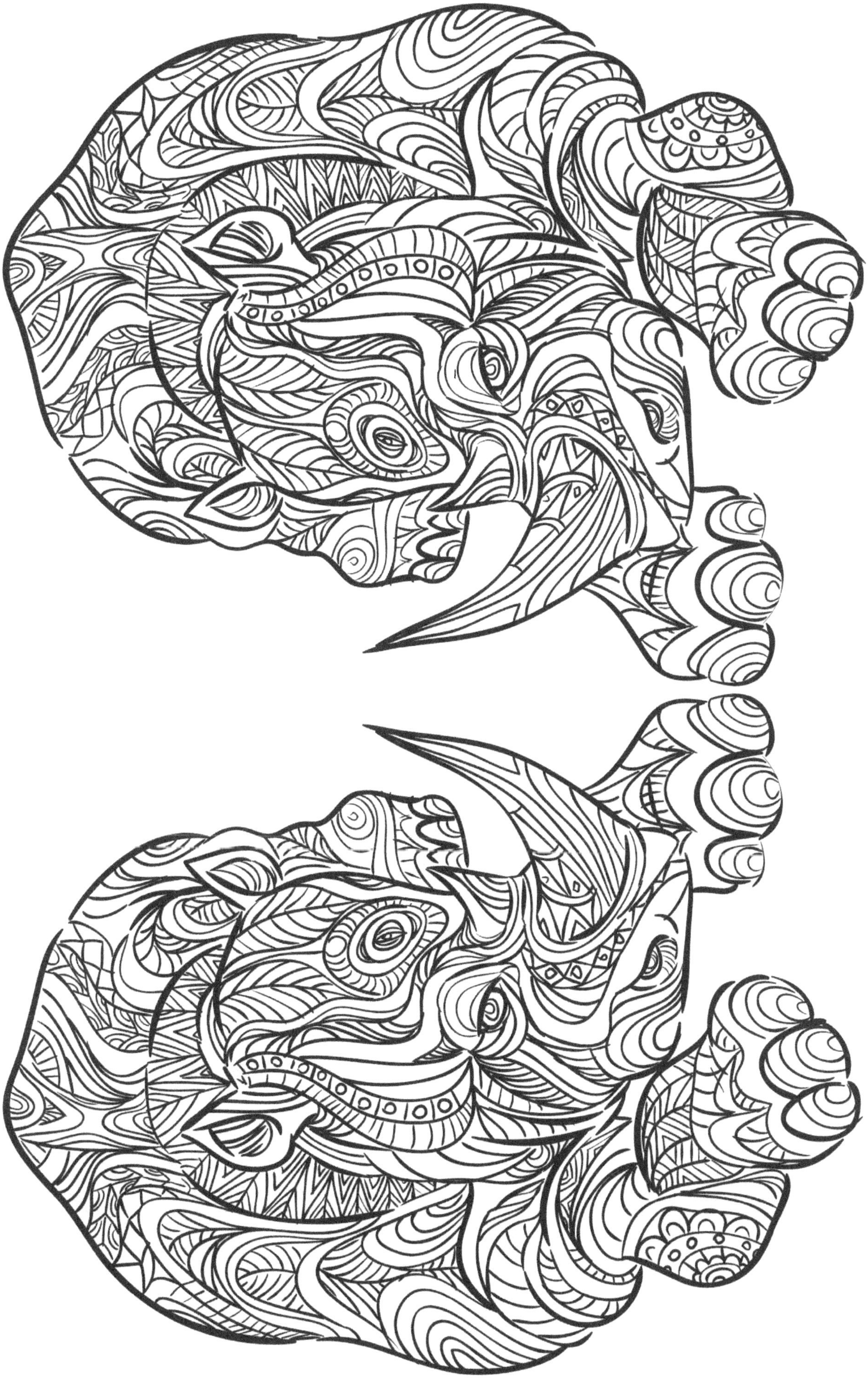

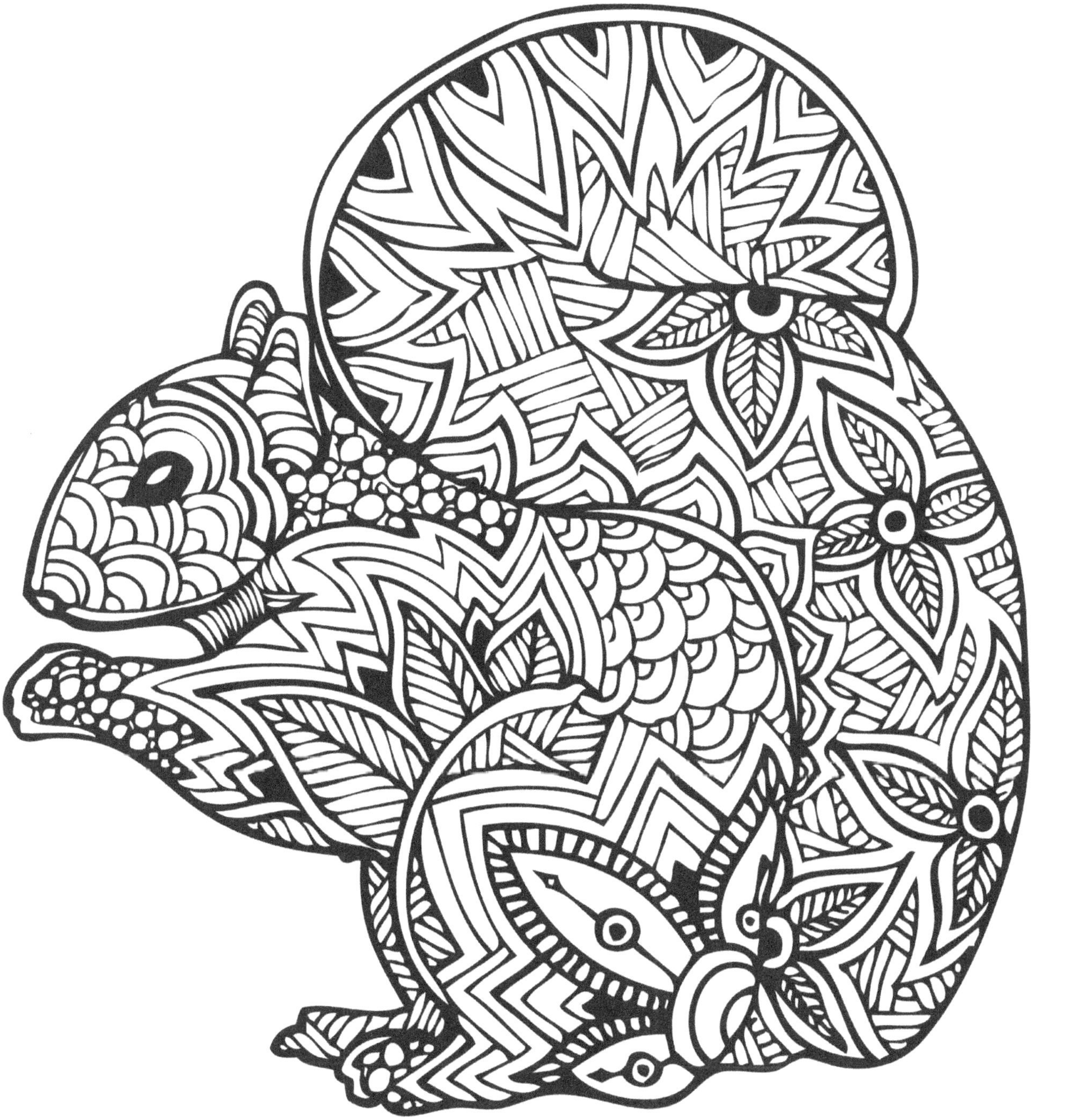

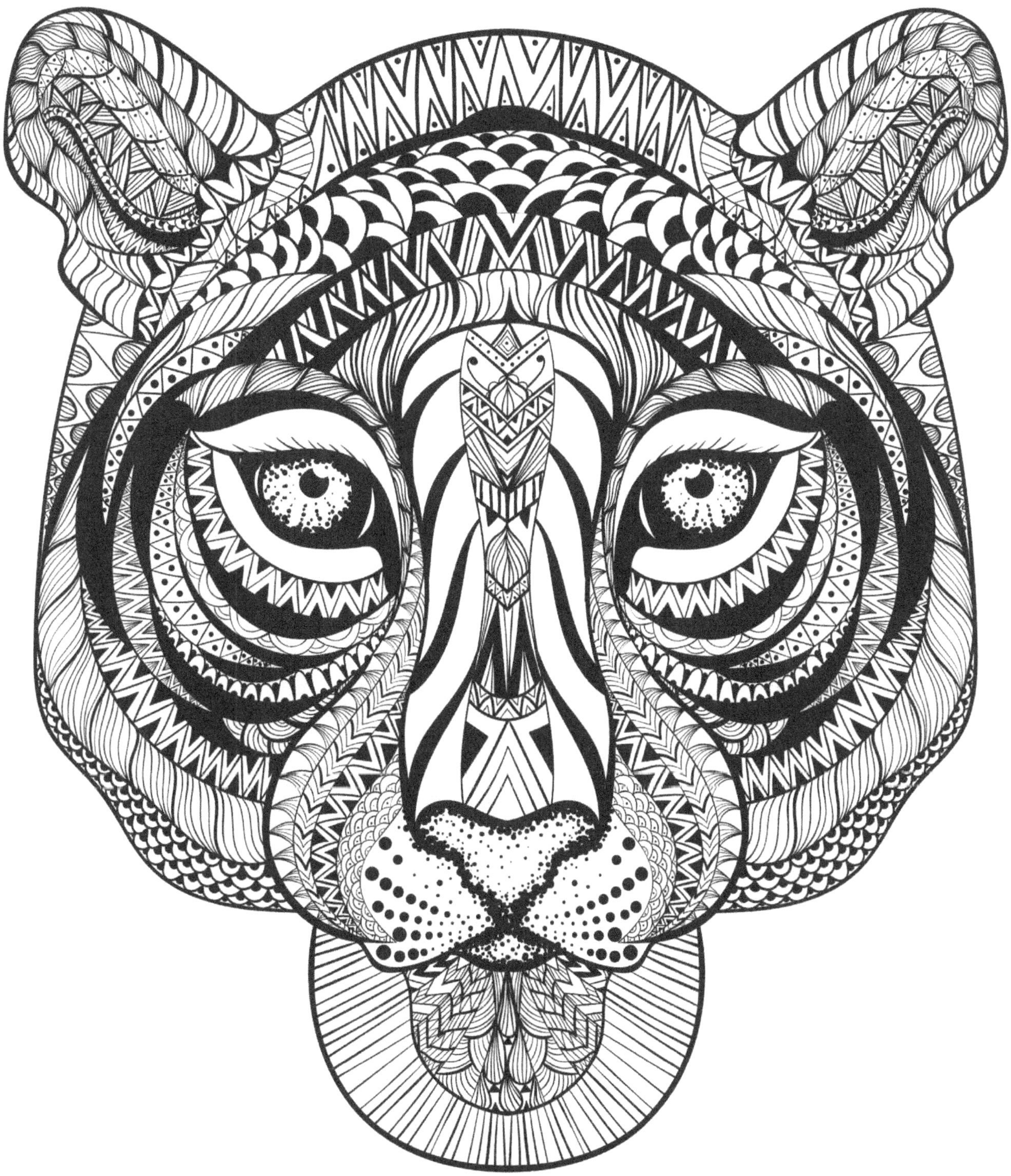

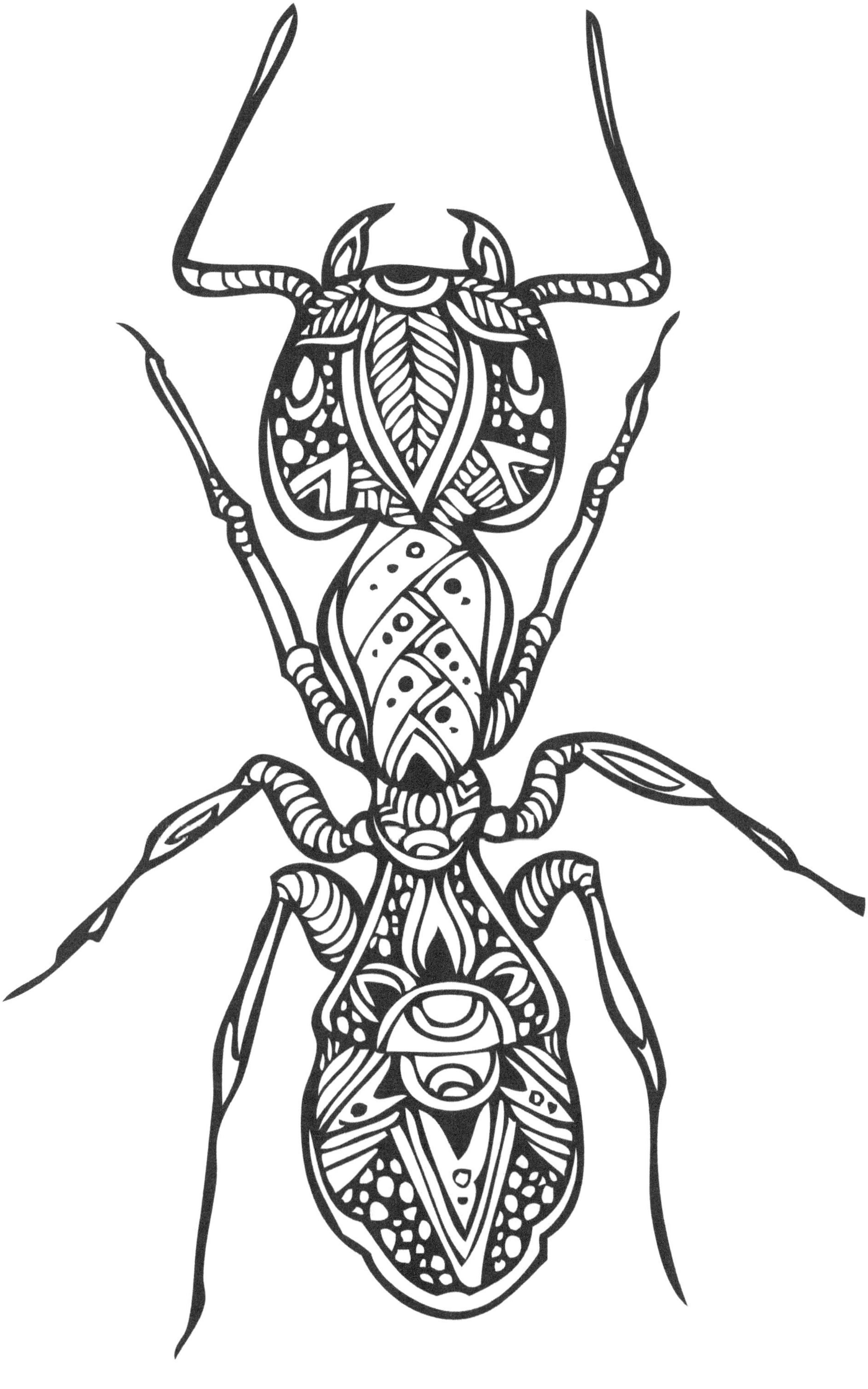

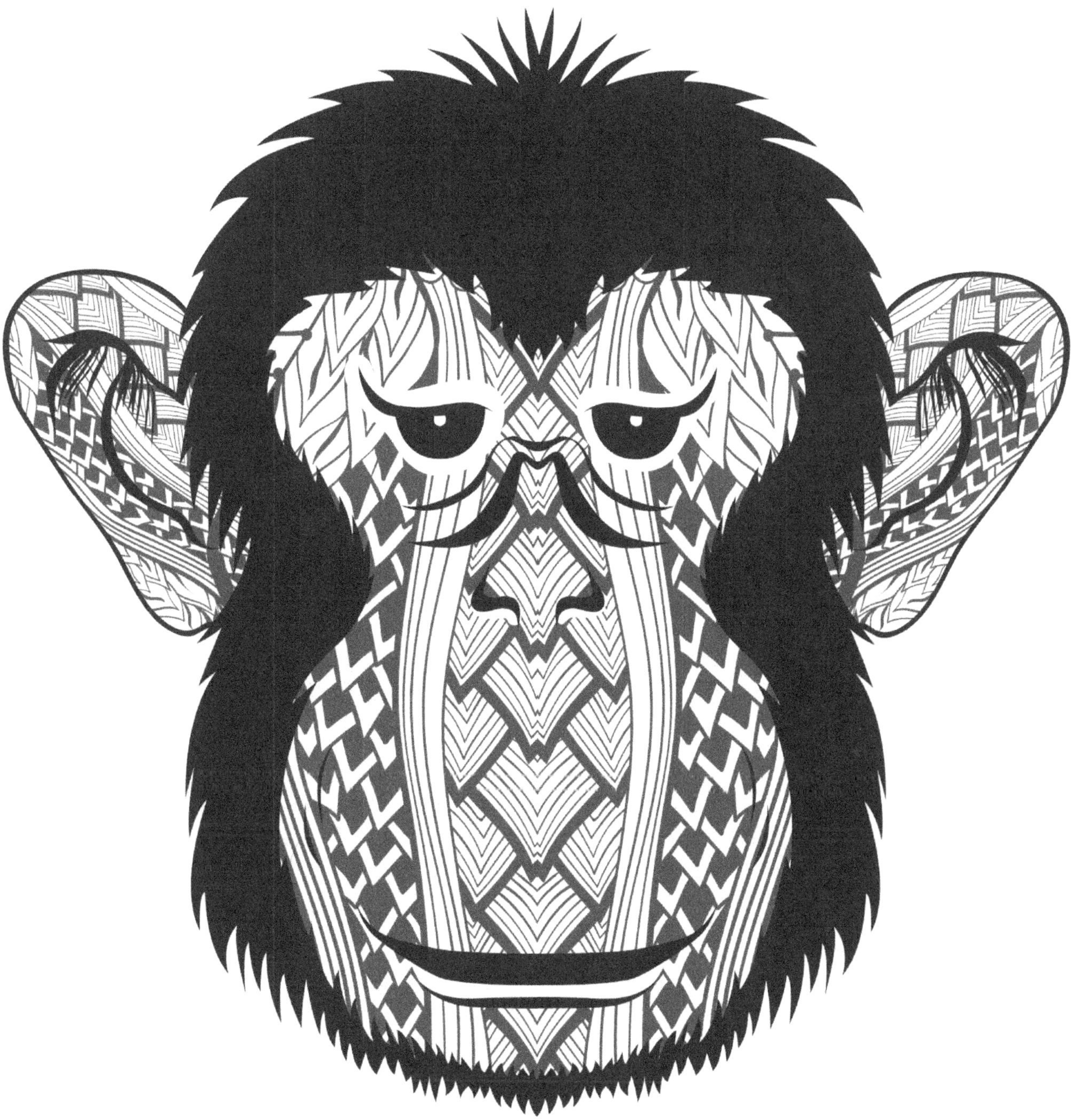

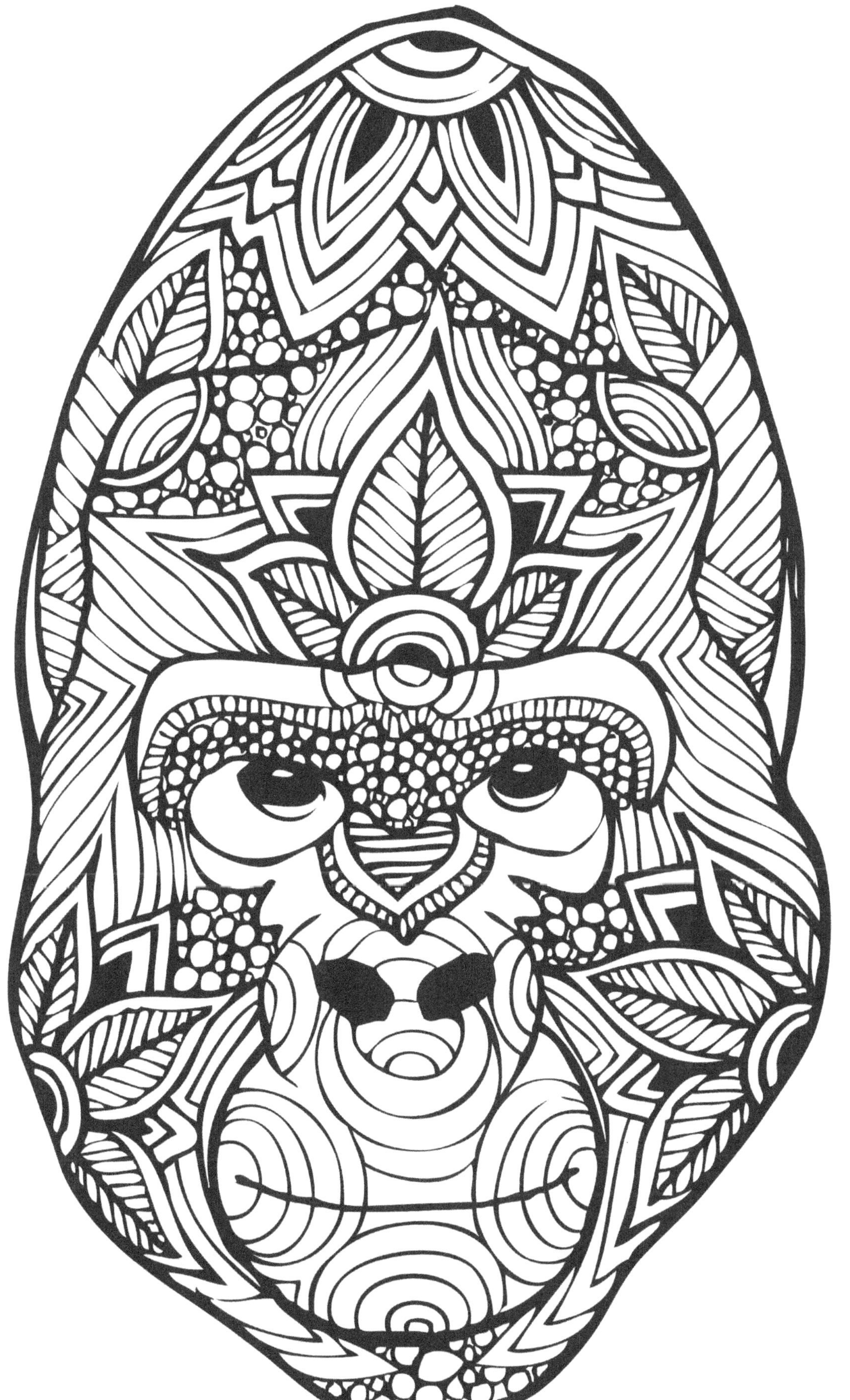

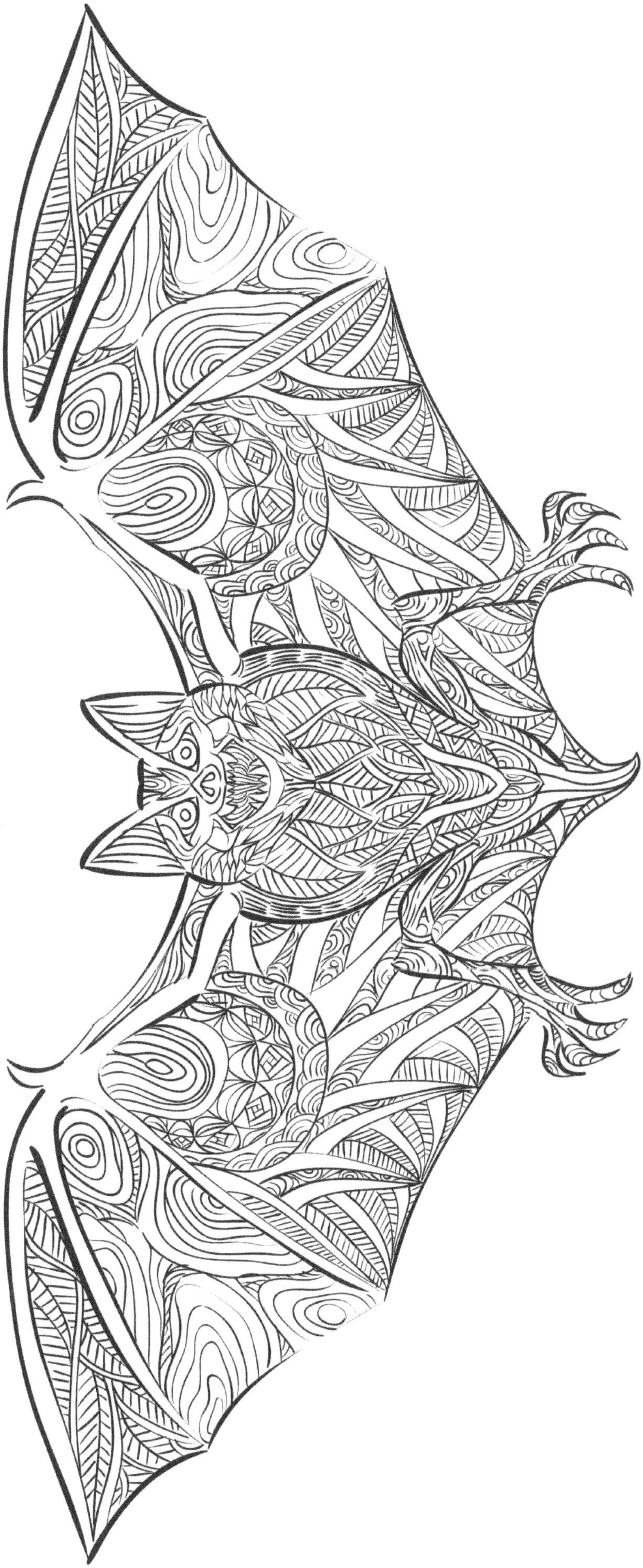

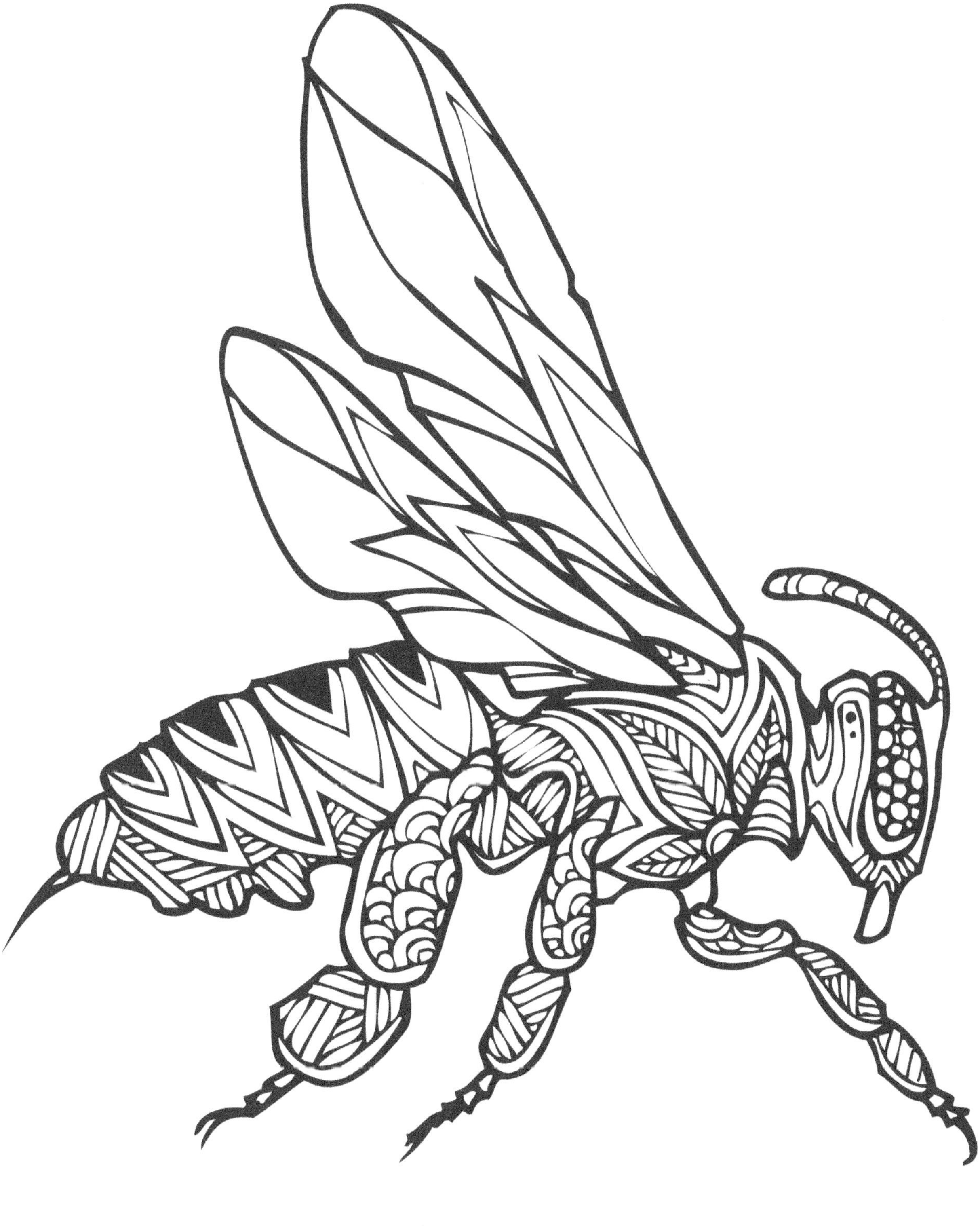

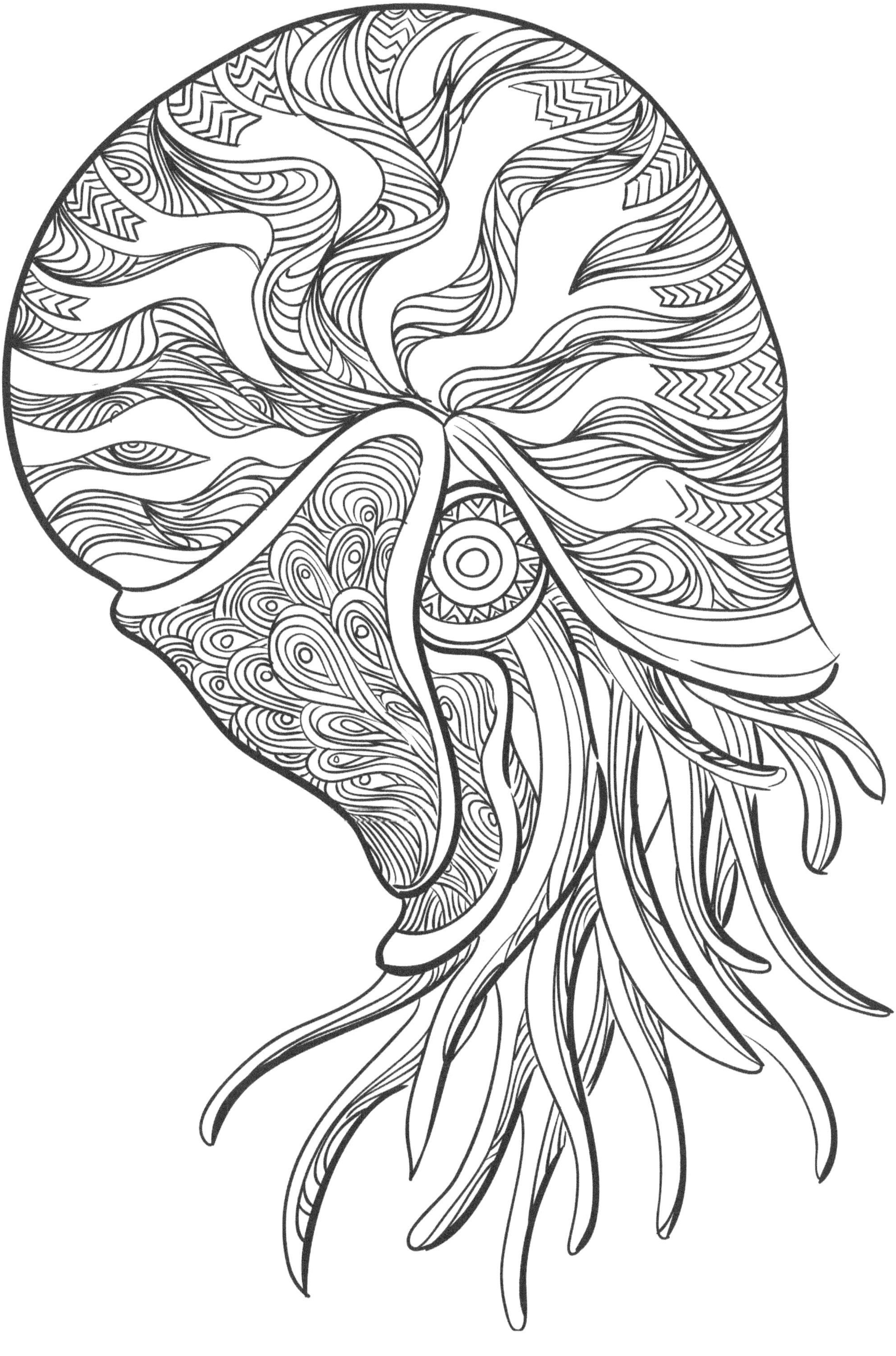

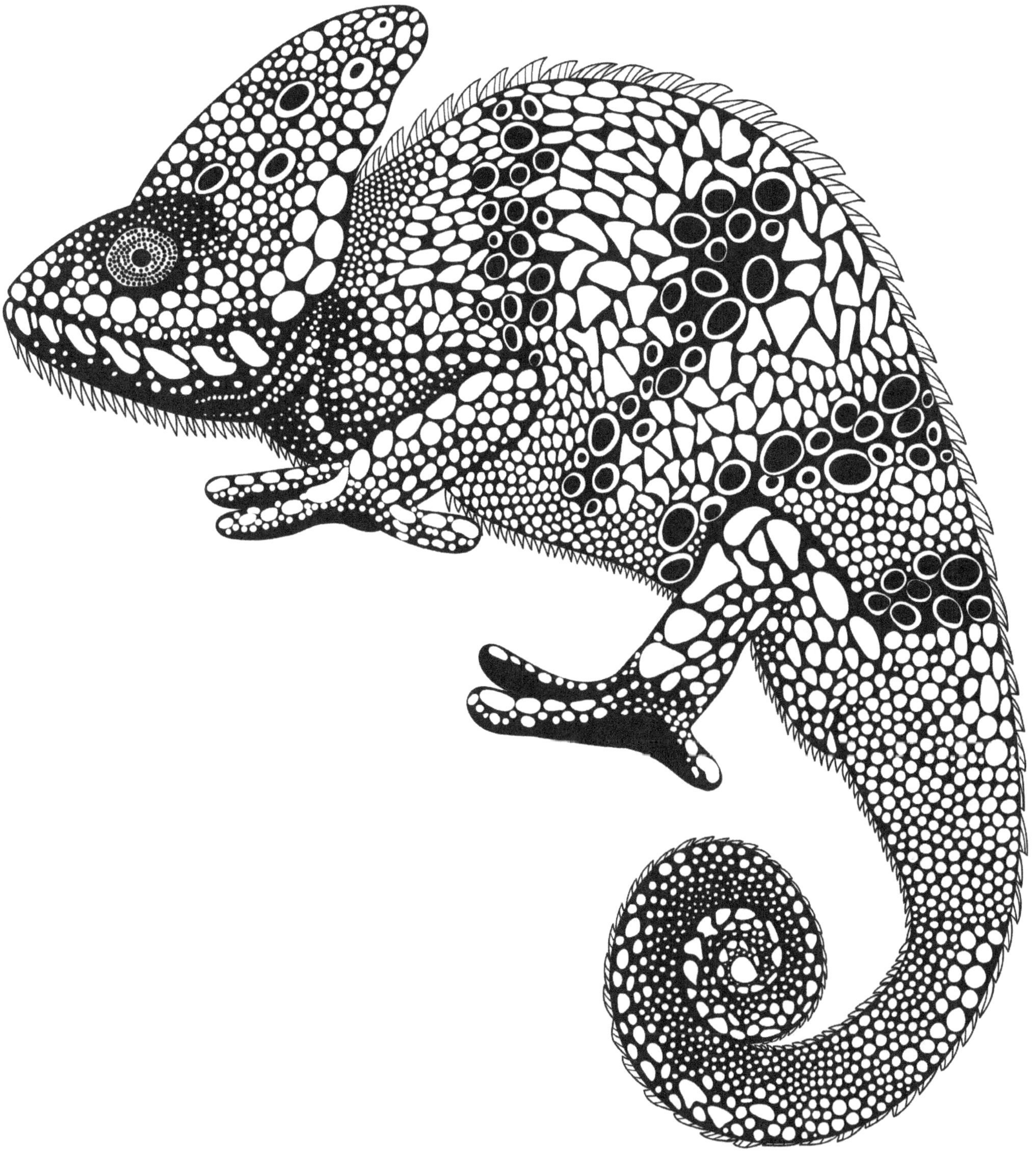

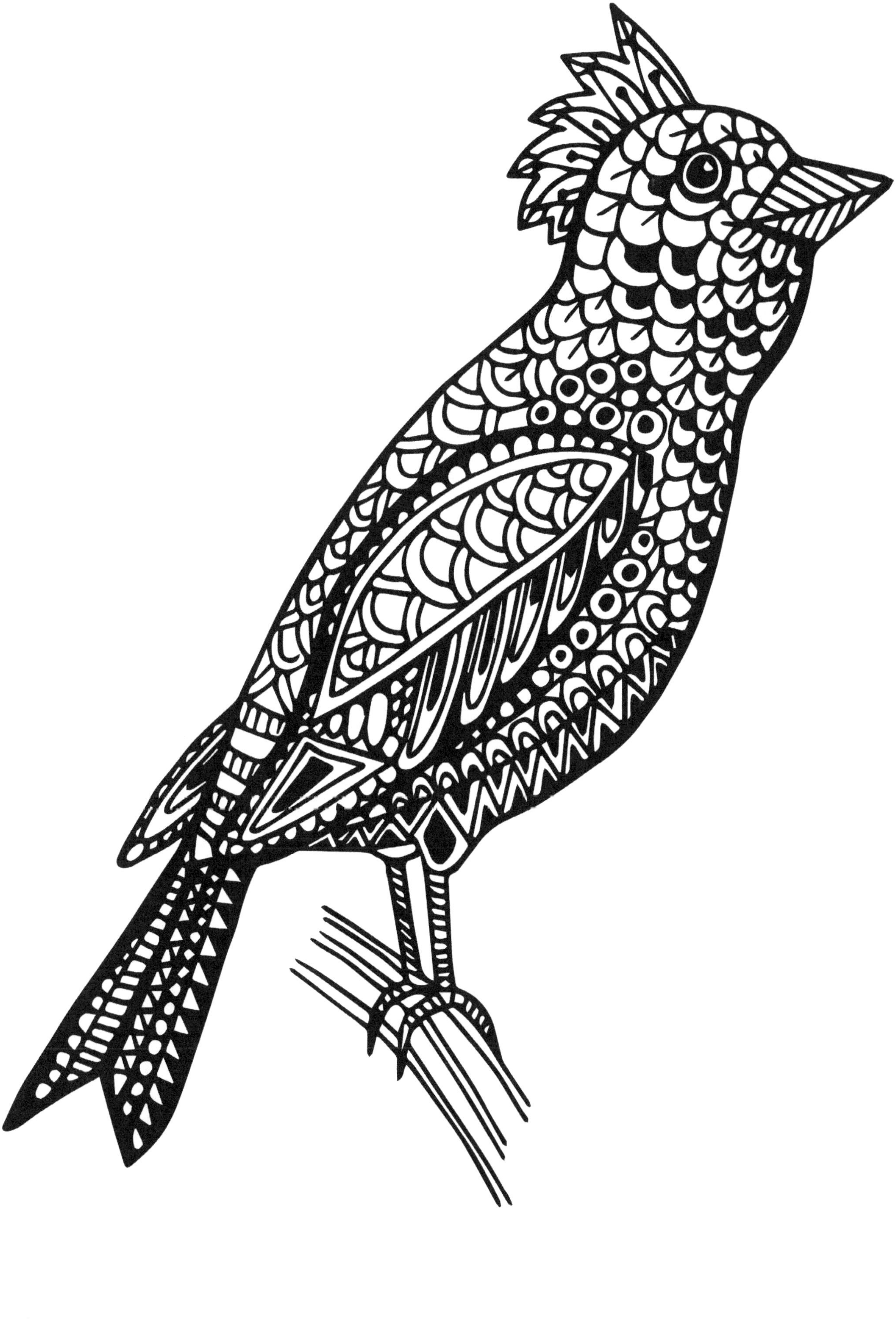

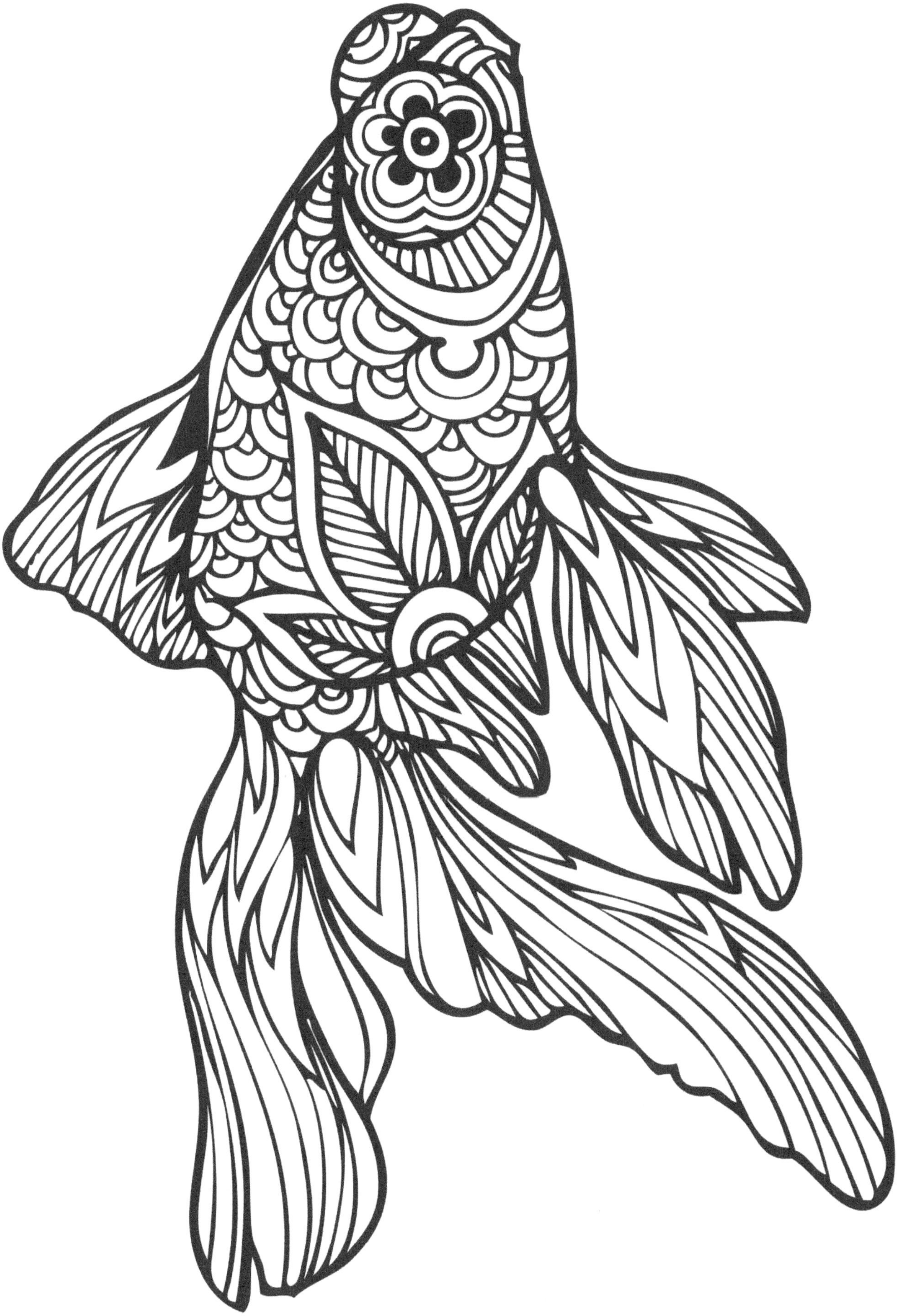

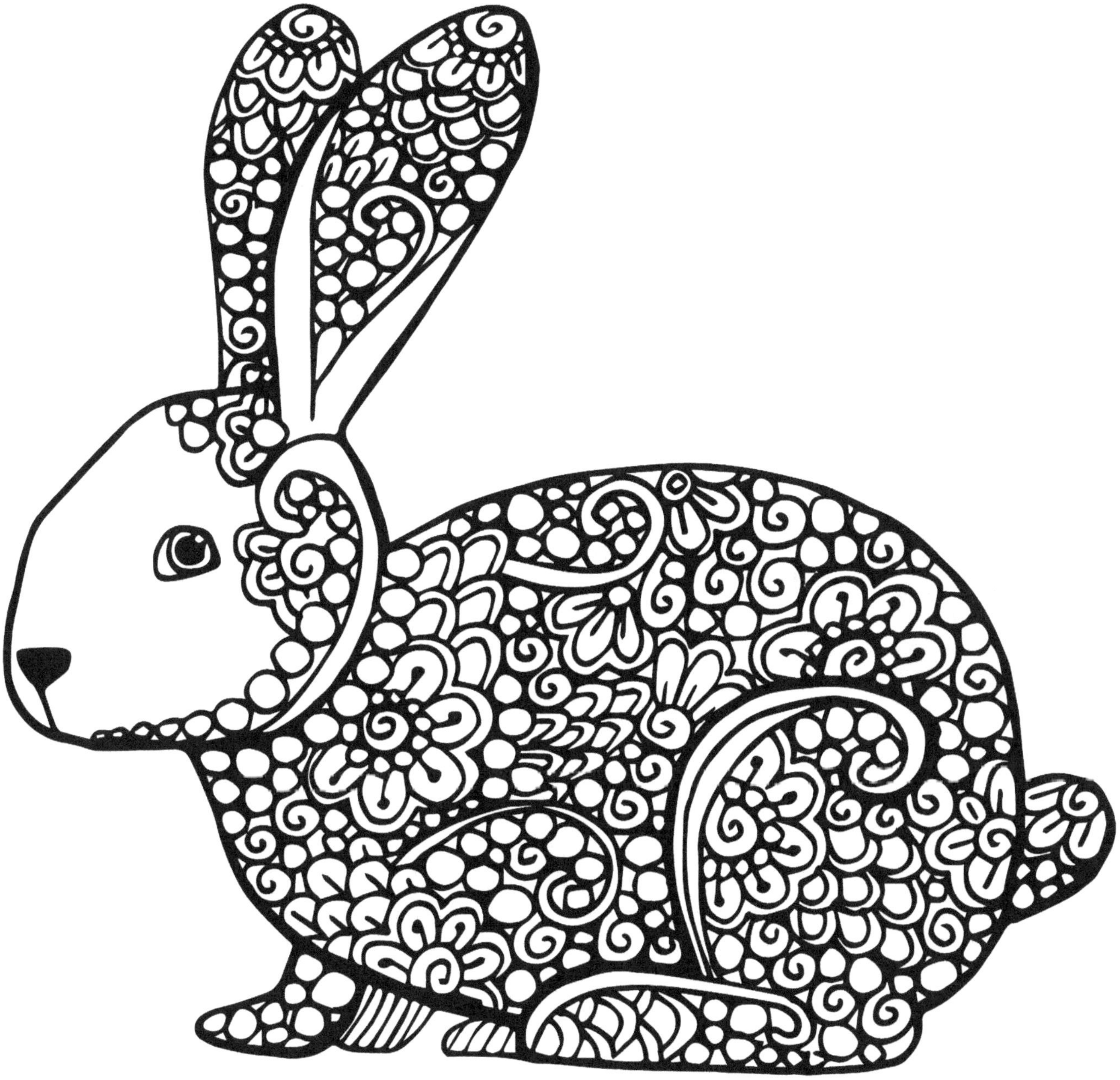

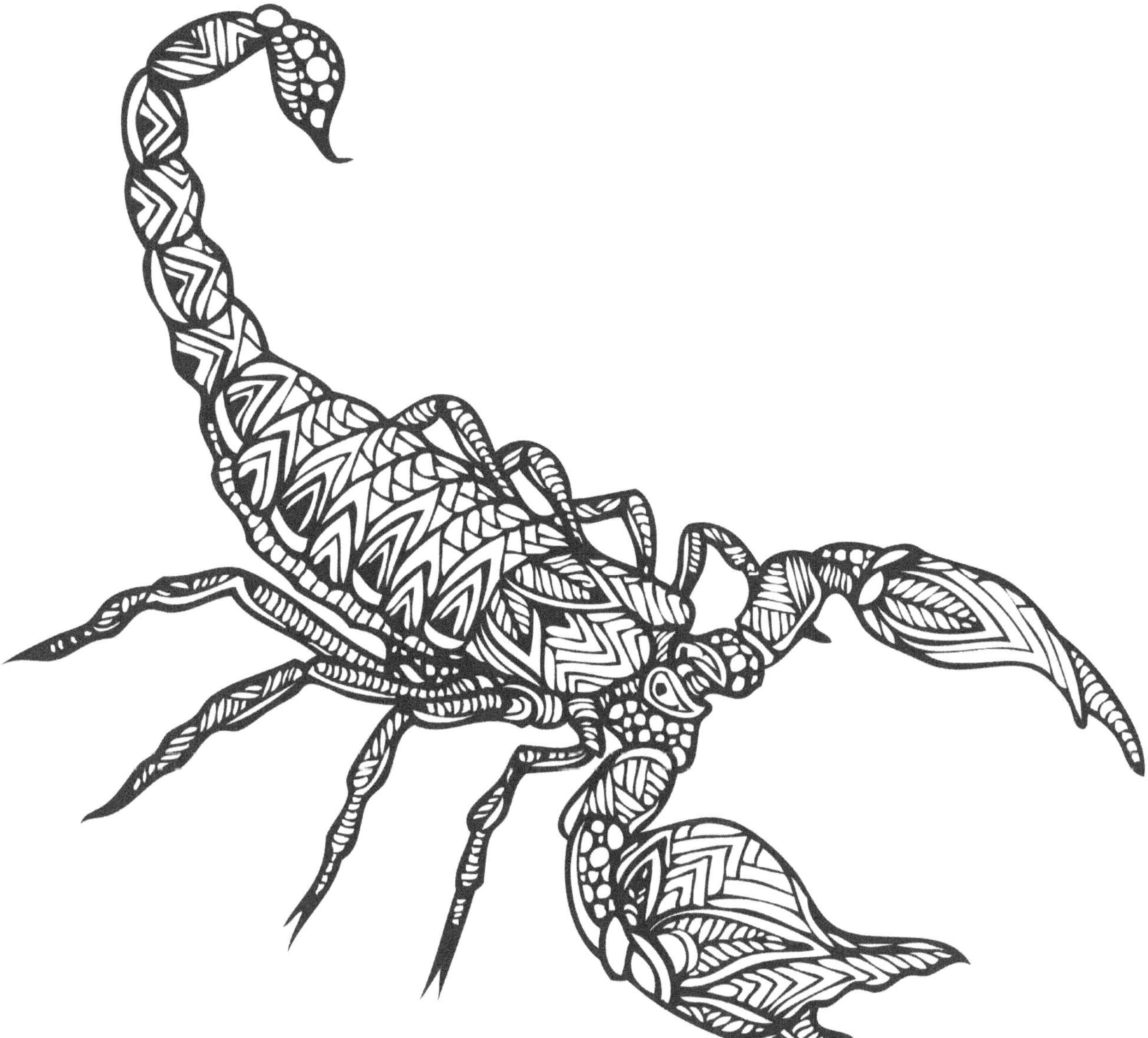

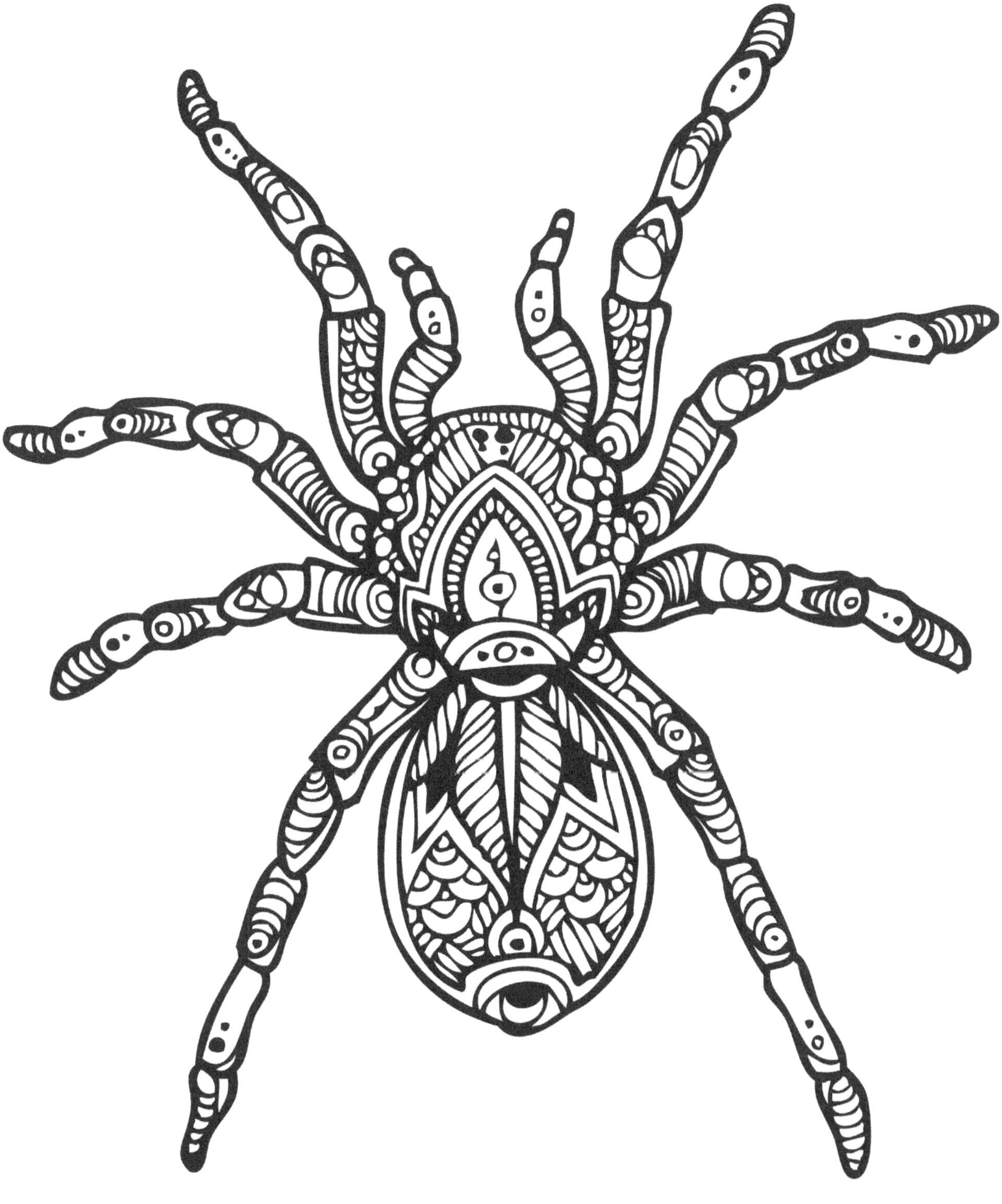

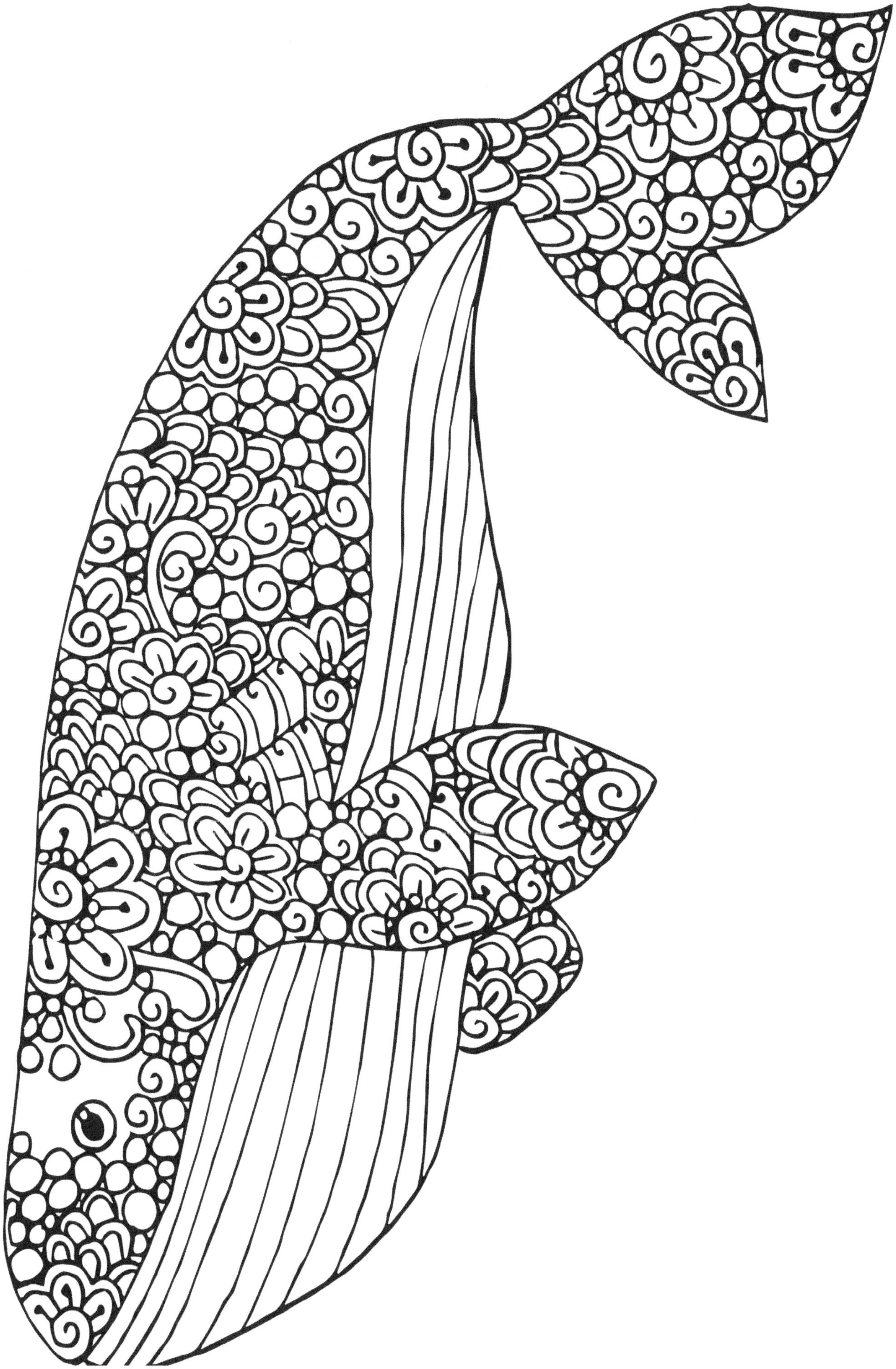

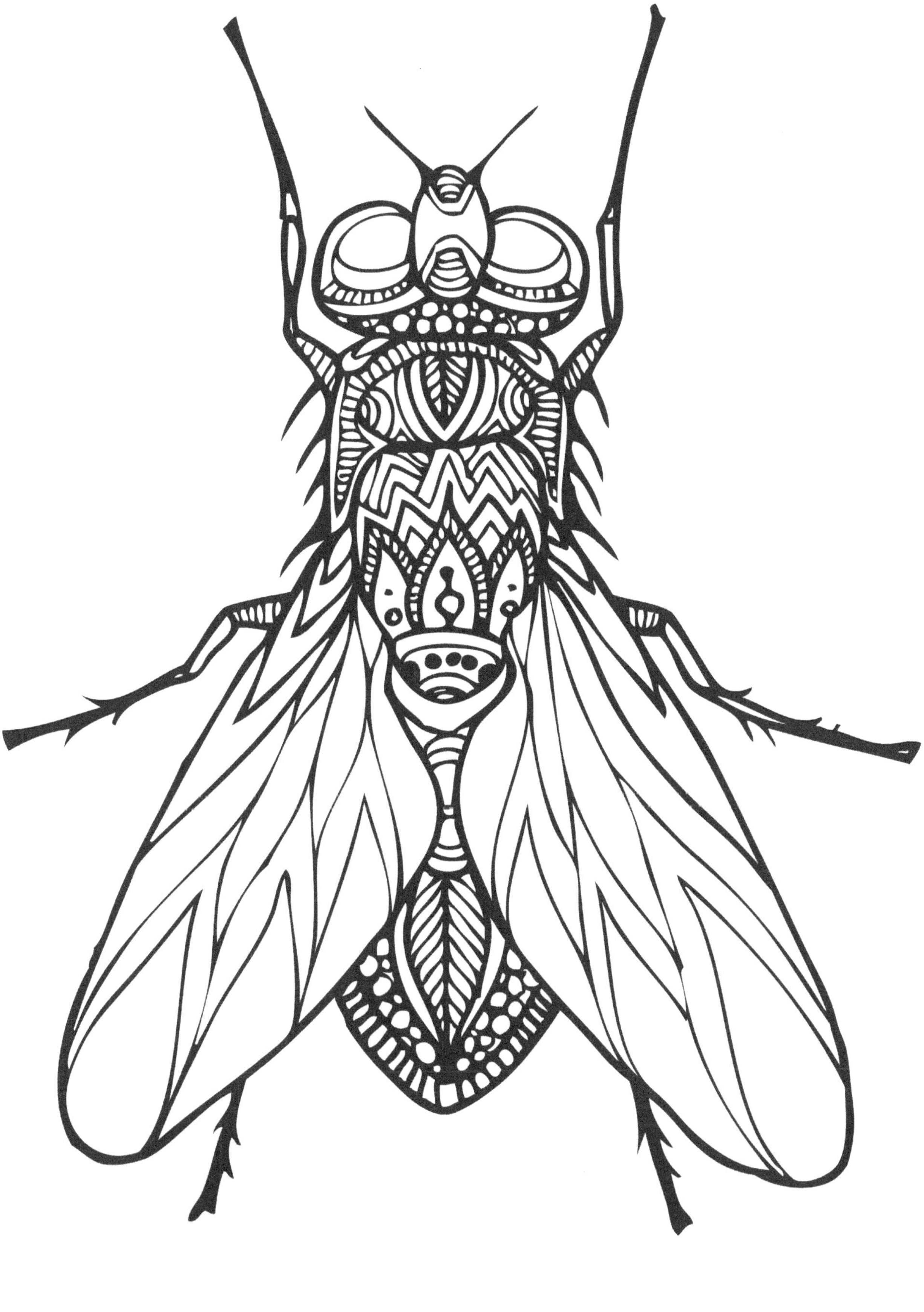

www.ingramcontent.com/pod-product-compliance
Lightning Source LLC
Chambersburg PA
CBHW080823180526
45168CB00006B/2552